what does it profit a man to gain
the whole world & lose his soul

ZEN
MILLIONAIRE

THE INVESTOR'S GUIDE TO THE "OTHER SIDE"

how to get rich in spirit & in fact
12 SECRETS

Paul B. Farrell, JD, PhD

First published by AuthorHouse 1/4/2007

ISBN: 978-1-4208-9652-7 (sc)

Library of Congress Control Number: 2005909881

Printed in the United States of America
Bloomington, Indiana

This book is printed on acid-free paper.

authorHOUSE™

1663 LIBERTY DRIVE, SUITE 200
BLOOMINGTON, INDIANA 47403
(800) 839-8640
WWW.AUTHORHOUSE.COM

to
The Next
ZEN MILLIONAIRE

Believe nothing,
no matter where you read it or who has said it,
not even if I have said it,
unless it agrees with your own reason
and your own common sense.
The Buddha

CONTENTS

ZEN MILLIONAIRE
The Formula for "Getting Rich in Spirit & in Fact"

This book is about you ....
About getting rich in fact *and in spirit*,
without selling your soul to the devil, CNBC, Wall Street.
It's about living by spiritual principles in a competitive world,
About realizing the American Dream with integrity.

Sixty years ago home ownership was the American Dream. Today we have a new American Dream—becoming a millionaire. Look at the statistics: We already have eight million American millionaires among ninety-five million investors. Another thirty million are working on that goal. That's a lot of 'millionaires-in-training' searching for the right path to this New American Dream.

Can you get rich in fact ... *and in spirit?*

How do you become a millionaire? Actually, the rules of the game are very simple. And yet, only one in three Americans are on the path. For many, the intangible costs are too high. Millions of Americans, however, face these conflicts head-on, balancing the demands of the commercial world with their spiritual convictions. How do you get rich in fact *and in spirit?* How can you become a millionaire without compromising your integrity? Without surrendering ethical, moral and spiritual principles? Without selling your soul to the devil?

The magical paradox of living successfully ... as a spiritual being in a material world

Over the past decade I've written about this new Zen Millionaire in a couple hundred of my columns on MarketWatch.com for CBS, DowJones and other online channels, and in nine books—and every time readers tell me they do know exactly what I'm talking about: The conflicts, struggles and daily choices they must make in a high-stressed, competitive world where values and principles often take a back seat to making a buck. This book is about how they do it—how these Zen Millionaires get rich in fact while growing rich in spirit.

Discover the Secret Path of the new Zen Millionaires and get rich in fact and in spirit .... without selling your soul to the devil, CNBC and Wall Street

OUL

meetings with

Wall Street's Mysterious

Zen Millionaire

*"What does it profit a man to gain the whole world
and suffer the loss of his soul?"*

The twelve principles in this book have been guiding a secret order of wealthy secular monks for two thousand years. They first learned these principles from a young wise man who traveled east from the Mediterranean along the trade routes to India, Tibet and China. For years this enlightened master taught monks of the Buddhist, Hindu and other faiths, challenging them to live by these principles *outside the protected walls of the monasteries without compromising their integrity, as spiritual beings in the material world.*

The challenge—getting rich in fact *and in spirit*

Those following this path were released of the vows of poverty and took up his challenge: "What does it profit a man to gain the whole world and suffer the loss of the soul?" Without the shelter of the monastery walls and disciplines, this new path became the ultimate test in their journey through life: *How to get rich in spirit and in fact, and enrich the world?*

They are not part of any formal religion, but rather a contradiction thriving outside traditional monastic isolation, like the Knights Templar. Now as then, they live and work quietly and prosperously in the fields of finance, business and industry throughout the world, in many cultures. Their twelve traditions have been passed on by word of mouth for centuries. They are the Zen Millionaires.

Meeting the Zen Millionaire on Wall Street

Back in the Seventies I met one of them in front of Morgan Stanley's headquarters. I had been working late and was exhausted, waiting for a cab, when a distinguished looking gentleman came out of the building and waved to me, "Hop in Paul, I'm headed for Soho, I'll give you a lift."

I was relatively new at Morgan Stanley, still feeling my way around the investment banking world. I thought he was a senior partner I should know. He looked familiar. He obviously knew me. We got in his limousine.

"The name's Matthew." He shook my hand. "Did you know Matthew was the patron saint of bankers, brokers, analysts and others in the finance business, even gamblers." Was he just making conversation? Or testing me, to see how I'd react? I tried not to look too puzzled. I nodded politely, figuring it best to listen. Let him do the talking until I remembered where I'd seen him.

How did he know I was headed for Soho, to a yoga meditation group? That was puzzling. I had never discussed it with anyone at the firm. Afraid they might think I was a bit too far-out for the conservative House of Morgan. That was before I learned that old J.P. Morgan himself was obsessed with astrology.

He asked about my interest in Zen, Taoism, Hopi shamanism, Sufism, the Quakers, Christian mysticism, Kabbalah, I-Ching, Tarot, and all the other spiritual paths I'd been quietly exploring since taking a seminar on Mythical Meditation with Joseph Campbell in Soho earlier in the year. The seminar was an epiphany that spun my life around completely, and left me questioning the meaning of my life, the meaning of all life. And made it possible to "see" the Zen Millionaire when he appeared.

After meeting Campbell everything suddenly looked different. The Zen Millionaire sensed it: "You have a 'beginner's mind,' a 'little monk' open to new ideas." At first I thought he was just being polite about my naivete. Or that he was much taller than me. Either way, he was a gentle soul who knew a lot about the world, about life, about me. And he had become my mentor. Today as I look back, I wonder: Was he real, or a projection of something deep within all of us?

Journeys into the "dark night of the soul'

He also knew that Hollywood was calling me, although it actually took a few years before I got the courage to let go of Wall Street. During that period he would appear every now and then, usually when I was working late, frustrated and deep in one of my dark-nights-of-the-soul moods. And with his wry, knowing smile he'd invite me into his world, inside the limousine, with its faint smell of burning incense. There as always some warm green tea, and his latest collection of spiritual icons.

During each of these trips to Soho I'd get another lesson about one of the twelve principles. I never did see him around the offices during the day. I kept my eyes open, curious, and asked about him. In time I stopped, I just accepted this mysterious gift, although his constant questioning was never easy. But in a strange way, I came to welcome them, expecting the unexpected, not sure when he'd appear next, but eagerly waiting for the next challenges he'd throw at me.

From Wall Street to Hollywood and beyond

Like most spiritual traditions, the way of the Zen Millionaire has been passed on from master to student in one-to-one meetings. I was fortunate to learn about his way, and challenged to live it. I was just a beginner, struggling to understand and live on this path, no big bank account, and constantly reminded of conflicts between principles and practice, ideals and reality. Eventually I did get to Hollywood and into the news media. He said it was time to go, urged me to continue on the path, wished me well, and said goodbye.

Then after years of silence, his limousine suddenly appeared one night as I left our CBS MarketWatch bureau offices on the West Coast. The "irrational exuberance" of the late nineties was peaking, the pendulum had swung far toward a materialistic extreme. He smiled, and offered me a ride. I was thrilled to see him. This time it was a hug rather than a handshake. Once again, he somehow knew I was headed for a group meditation meeting that evening. But by now all his unusual insights into me and the world seemed quite normal.

In search of a new moral compass

He said he came with a request: It was time to get the message out to a wider audience, to tell people about the principles, to speak from the heart, in my own voice, using my experiences. That's when I began writing about the way of the Zen Millionaire, over a hundred columns on CBS MarketWatch, later DowJones MarketWatch and the Wall Street Journal.

Something quite fascinating happened after the initial columns outlined the twelve principles—investors began telling me how they were already working in their lives.

Somehow investors already knew what I was talking about, knew it at a gut level and were *already living this way even before they read about it, as if the message were passed on, no longer by individual masters in one-on-one meetings, but by a universal intelligence through what Carl Jung called the 'collective unconscious'* that links each of us at a deep soul level, very real, though difficult to label on a practical level.

Focus on what you are *for,* not what you are *against*

The Zen Millionaire appeared one last time a few years later, before he passed away. He was concerned about the extreme imbalances in the world—cultural conflicts, global wars and terrorism, mounting domestic challenges to financial markets and the economy, the future of individuals worldwide. He said many of his old Wall Street friends had lost their way. Greed was consuming them, was systemic throughout the industry.

At that moment, however, he was more concerned about what all this was doing to me—he warned me about "focusing on what you're against, rather that what you are for. Fight them and you're playing their game by their rules. Then you become one of them, in danger of losing your soul, your way."

He had been reading my columns on CBS MarketWatch the past decade and later on Dow Jones, the Wall Street Journal and other sources. He was well aware that in recent years I had become an investigative journalist, exposing corporate and mutual fund scandals, writing about the widespread "conspiracy," as Vanguard's founder Jack Bogle called it, between Congress, the SEC, the White House sabotaging reforms through special interest lobbyists hired by Wall Street and Corporate America. He could see that I was caught up in fighting these battles—playing their game, by their rules, on their playing field.

Play their game, by their rules—they will win

Then he became quite serious and reached for several of my columns that he apparently had in his briefcase. He began flipping through them in rapid fire, reading highlighted sections: "You quote Peter Fitzgerald, the senator who drafted the Mutual Fund Reform Act that was later killed by the conspiracy: 'The mutual fund industry is now the world's largest skimming operation, a $7 trillion trough from which fund managers, brokers and other insiders are steadily siphoning off an excessive slice of the nation's household, college and retirement savings' ... here's Arthur Levitt, former SEC chairman saying, 'America's investors have been ripped off as massively as a bank being held up by a guy with a gun and a mask.' ... another by Jack Bogle who's been calling the fund industry a 'casino' for decades, telling us 'the croupier is skimming a third off the average fund win.' ... here's Morningstar's boss, Don Phillip, 'the fund industry has lost its moral compass.' ... you mention David Swensen, the incredibly successful manager of Yale Endowment Fund, saying: 'The colossal failure of the mutual fund industry carries serious implications for society, etcetera, etc.' That's quite an indictment ... You also wrote often about behavioral finance experts like Princeton psychologist Daniel Kahneman, who won the Nobel prize in economics for research proving that investors are irrational and Wall Street's 'rational investor' theory is a only a myth ... Yes, all this is true, Paul ... it's a well-known fact that America's 95 million investors are no match for industry pros ... as Swensen put it rather bluntly; 'Individual investors lose. Mutual fund managers win' every time."

But they still run the casino, still control the game!

"Powerful critics: Senators, SEC chairman, Vanguard's founder, Nobel economist, Morningstar's boss, Yale University's money manager ... *But so what? The Wall Street Conspiracy still runs the casino, the trillion dollar fund industry, controls all the assets belonging to America's 95 million individual investors. They still control the game, the rules, all the players ... and now you!"*

"How? Simple. Because Wall Street and the fund managers have an extremely well-funded special interest lobby. They control the SEC, Congress, and the White House. Everything they do is cleverly orchestrated to protect the billions they are secretly skimming off the top of your retirement funds."

Only way to win—play your game, by your rules

"They're winning the game whenever you're fighting them on their turf ... so they win, you lose, every time ... get it? You're still playing their game ... by their rules ... not your game by your rules ... you're distracted, frustrated, vulnerable, right where they want you ... and worse yet, Paul, you're not involved in something that's positive, inspiring and fulfilling ... you're off your game, you're off the path ... and you are not helping people that way ... the time for reform and revolution will come, but for now, there are forces driving the markets, the economy and the government that are far more powerful than you and any of these critics. Eventually the conspiracy will self-destruct of its own—*don't you go down with it.*"

He stopped, quietly staring at me, as his message sunk in. Another epiphany as he slowly began tearing up my columns, one at a time.

"Get back on the path Paul. Let others fight against the darkside. You must look inside, refocus," his finger tapped my forehead, "reprogram your brain, it's time, now!

Powerful new network—the collective conscience

"There's a grassroots network emerging, millions of investors all quietly thinking like you and me." He put his hand over my heart: "This collective conscience connects all of us into one network, all connected to the universal mind, connected with each other, and connected with you. Listen to the still small voice. There is a Creator guiding you and everyone in this network. Write about it. Help investors to see, to think, to act in a whole new way about their money, about investing, retirement ... and the meaning of life."

His challenge: "Tell people about all we've discussed over the years, our ancient traditions, the twelve principles, your experience with them. And when your words fall short, trust the wisdom of the masters. The truth is constant throughout history, it has been repeated over and over by far wiser folks than you and me. Now's the time. Say it eloquently or awkwardly if you have to—but pass it on."

PART ONE

THE ZEN
OF
GETTING RICH
IN SPIRIT & IN FACT

Early in life our values and principles come from family. Later we learn how they fit together ourselves. For me, they came from many sources over many years; the 10 commandments, the Boy Scouts, the U. S Marine Corps, the 12-Step spiritual program, and many less structured sources such as the trauma of childhood abandonment, a doctorate in transformational psychology, even a few months farming at the Esalen Institute in the Big Sur, to name a few.

The single biggest life-changing experience for me occurred at midlife, in a seminar on Mythical Meditation given by Joseph Campbell, author of *The Hero of a Thousand Faces, The Journey of The Hero*, and many others. He opened my eyes to two traditions from very different worlds, the Western psychology of Carl Jung, and Zen tradition of the East. Both teach us to rely on first-hand experience in the search for the truth, to trust our inner voices, and to learn by doing, experimenting, and making mistakes. Campbell made it possible for me to see the Zen Millionaire on Wall Street.

In the Zen way there is no dependence on second-hand experience and third-party dogma filtered through gurus, clerics, pundits, and outside authority figures. Zen has nothing to do with organized religions, nor any other "isms" that require you to turn your mind over to someone else. The secret power is within you. The kingdom is within. What you are looking for, you are looking with. You are it. Listen. There is no separation between you and your higher power, between you and the world, between your money and your spirit. The Zen Millionaire helped me realize that I already knew all this, from long ago— that it was encoded in my genes, and yours.

First Secret

YOU GET THE
ZEN FIRST
BEFORE THE MILLION BUCKS

All the other principles flow from this first one. You get it, or you got nothing. Being a Zen Millionaire means thinking like one, today, now, *before you have the million bucks.* In fact, you're probably a long way from having a million dollar nest egg, maybe decades. You aren't "there," but you are on the path, working toward the money, *and you got the Zen.*

In short, you get the Zen first, before you get the million bucks, you get into action and you live by these principles, in the present, every day. You can be in any business, practice any religion, live anywhere—you get the Zen first. What is it? Very simple: As martial arts champion Chuck Norris says in *The Secret Power Within: Zen Solutions to Real Problems:*

> **Zen is not about monks meditating as much as it is about taking action, making decisive moves in the present. There's a certain impatience about Zen, an unwillingness to get lost in meandering arguments, a desire to cut quickly to the essential, or to 'get to the bottom line.'**

Another great Zen teacher, Alan Watts, described this elusive mystery in even simpler terms: "Zen is all that side of life which is complete beyond our control." What an odd paradox: You're totally responsible for the bottom line … yet the bottom line is beyond your control! Here's how The Boss, rock star Bruce Springsteen put this

3

strange puzzle in a different context that anyone can understand:

You've got to be able to hold a lot of contradictory ideas in your mind without going nuts. I feel like to do my job right, when I walk out onstage I've got to feel like it's the most important thing in the world. Also I've got to feel like, well, it's only rock and roll. Somehow you've got to believe both of those things.

Get that and you're a winner going in this game! You handle ambiguity with a positive mental attitude, even in the worst of circumstances. Here's how a U.S. Special Forces instructor with 26 years experience described this ability in a *Fast Company* magazine:

If you have a guy with all the survival training in the world who has a negative attitude and a guy who doesn't have a clue but has a positive attitude, I guarantee you that the guy with a positive attitude is coming out of the woods alive. Simple as that.

Zen is more than the familiar positive mental attitude, but it's a great starting point. So what's the biggest challenge you'll face? Just this: How to find the "meaning of life" in this time of prosperity, before and after you are a have a million dollars? When you have all the money you need and more? When you get "there," will it be worth the price?

How do you get rich in spirit and in fact? How do you gain the whole world and feed your soul too? That's the ultimate challenge for you—discovering the *meaning of your life every step of the way*. And that is far more important than getting the money first.

Millionaire-in-training with a "Zen mind"

Check the facts: Statistically we already know most Americans don't have their million bucks sitting in the bank. There are only eight million Americans who have a million dollar net worth, out of more than 300 million people. And among them, less than a third are what you'd call "millionaires-in-training" folks saving and investing enough to become a millionaire down the road.

Most of you are probably a very long way from having a million dollar net worth statement, maybe two or three decades away. And you could be the late-blooming boomer who's starting late, finally putting some money in a savings plan, or better yet, getting into a business, investing in yourself. Or you could be a twenty-year-old college sophomore with a single stock or mutual fund.

So yes, we know that at the start you aren't "there" yet. It's okay not to have the million dollars net worth sitting in the bank. Start where you are now, be a Zen Millionaire in spirit. You get the Zen first.

But the key is, you're on the path, working for it. That's what really counts, *you are taking responsibility and into action.* In other words, you get the Zen first—get centered in a secret power within you—before you get the million bucks. You are already a Zen Millionaire, in spirit!

Enlightenment first? Or a million bucks?

All the other principles flow from this first principle, get in the Zen way of living and you got the secret. Being a Zen Millionaire requires a new way of thinking, of seeing, of being in the world. The delightful Zen teacher Shunryu Suzuki tells us about this challenge in his classic, *Zen Mind, Beginner's Mind:*

> **Which is more important; to attain enlightenment, or to attain enlightenment before you attain enlightenment; to make a million dollars, or to enjoy your life in your effort, little by little, even though it is impossible to make a million; to be successful, or to find some meaning in your effort to be successful.**

The journey is the answer, the path, the way—the journey. *You must find the meaning in the journey, your journey. And y*ou must learn to enjoy it, get into action to the fullest, and live it with honor and integrity. You must grasp the meaning, the happiness, along the way—*not later, when you arrive, when you have the million* *bucks, but now, today, this very moment!* Long before you have the money.

The path—hidden in plain sight

The path of the Zen Millionaire is not hidden in some cosmic esoteric philosophy. It won't take you years to discover. Quite the contrary, it is simple, obvious, immediate, personal and easy to grasp—if you choose to see it. Martial arts champion Chuck Norris put it simple and direct in *The Secret Power Within: Zen Solutions to Real Problems:*

> **One of the basic tenets of Zen is that it really has nothing at all to teach, nothing to say: According to Zen, the truth is obvious, or should be. The truth is nothing that can be taught. You can't sit down at a desk and wait for a lecturer to step up to the podium and reveal the truth to you. Instead, you have to become aware of it on your own.**

What will you discover? Very simple: Within you are all the hidden resources you'll ever need. All the great events of the world, the great transformations begin with you, the individual—*you can and will make the difference.*

A sacred agreement—your life's mission

The Zen way of seeing and being in the world means that you go deep into that inner silence, deep within you, and talk to the inner being there with you—*your soul*—where you discover the answer to a simple challenge tossed at you and me, the millionaire-next-door and everybody else by the physicist and former Special Forces soldier Gary Zukav in *The Seat of The Soul:*

> **Each soul comes to the Earth with gifts. A soul does not incarnate only to heal and to balance its energy, to pay its karmic debts, but also to contribute its specialness in specific ways ... Before it incarnates,**

each soul agrees to perform certain tasks upon Earth. It enters into a sacred agreement with the Universe to accomplish specific goals … Whatever the task your soul has agreed to, whatever its contract with the Universe, all of the experiences of your life serve to awaken within you the memory of that contract, and to prepare you to fulfill it.

So once again, please take a moment and ask yourself: What is the meaning of your life? What is your task? Your contract? Your gifts to give? Your mission this life? Why did you come here? *Who are you?*

"What is Zen?" Open your eyes—no mystery

We are all asking the same questions. At the level of soul you, me, all of us are searching for answers. That's what life's about, a search for the meaning of life, where the question is more important than the answer. And most of the time we are asking the wrong question. In *Man's Search for Meaning* the psychiatrist and holocaust survivor Viktor Frankl tells you to shift your thinking, ask the right question:

"It did not really matter what we expected from life, but rather what life expected from us. We needed to stop asking about the meaning of life, and instead to think of ourselves as those who were being questioned by life— daily and hourly. Our answer must consist, not in talk and meditation, but in right action and right conduct. Life ultimately means taking the responsibility to find the right answers to its problems and to fulfill the tasks which it constantly sets for each individual. The tasks, and therefore the meaning of life, differ from man to man, and from moment to moment."

No questioning? No responsibility? Then no Zen! You must discover the answers—*your* answers, then get into action. Just keep it simple, there are no grand sweeping gestures in Zen, for as Suzuki reminds us in elegant simplicity:

There is, after all, nothing mysterious in Zen. Everything is open to you in full view. If you eat your food and keep yourself cleanly dress and work on the farm to raise your rice or vegetables, you are doing all that is required of you on this earth, and the infinite is realized in you.

Remember, all principles flow from this first principle. Being a Zen Millionaire demands a new way of seeing and thinking and being— but most of all, remember, *you get the Zen first, before you get the million bucks.*

And if you do get the million bucks first, without the Zen, you are still left with the nagging question from the good book: "What does it profit a man to gain the whole world and suffer the loss of his soul?" And for many, the answers are harder to find after getting the million dollars. *Take care of the soul first, and, paradoxically, you will gain the whole world.*

The road less traveled—leads to a million bucks

Money alone will never provide meaning to your life. Deep within, you already know this is true. Dr. Peck summarized this truth rather bluntly in *The Road Less Traveled and Beyond:*

What constitutes wealth? In worldly terms, it is the possession of money and valuable things. But if we were to measure wealth in other ways, besides mere dollars, many who are poor in possessions are spiritually rich, and many who own much are spiritually impoverished.

You know this: You know you must get the Zen first before you get the million bucks because deep within you, you know that you are not just a human being having spiritual experiences. Rather, you are in the words of the philosopher Teilhard de Chardin, "a spiritual being having human experiences."

You have no choice. This you know. This you must live with, all day, every day. Act in a contrary way and your conscience, your spirit, your inner gyroscope will send uncomfortable warning signals—you will be left with a feeling of being incomplete, split, not your true self.

First a millionaire in spirit—the spirit of Zen

Deep in their soul every Zen Millionaire-in-training already knows what all of this means—*instinctively*—and is struggling to live by this principle, walking the talk. It is the beginning and the end of the journey, the shift in our thinking, the first and the last step our Zen teacher Suzuki wants us to finally grasp:

Without being aware of it, we try to change something other than ourselves, we try to order things outside ourselves. But it is impossible to organize things if you are not in order. When you do things in the right way, at the right time, everything else will be organized. You are the 'boss.' When the boss is sleeping, everyone is sleeping.

In the Zen Millionaire's way of life, you are the boss, you are in charge, you control your priorities, you are responsible, period. And while you're on this long journey, you'll find the meaning of your life, fulfill your task, and discover who you are.

NEW MINDSET
YOUR MIND
CREATES
THE MONEY

Zen is a state of mind, a new way of thinking. So is being a millionaire-in-training. Yin and yang. The monk and the samurai. Receptive and aggressive. Combine the two opposites within you, and you will tap into the secret power of the universe.

You are the creator, you know the mind creates money. Your mind is creating the million bucks—you are a money machine. The money is already yours because the money is already in the flow of creation, moving from the universal mind through your mind, into reality. You dream, your mind creates. The philosopher George Bernard Shaw saw it this way:

Some men see things as they are, and say, 'Why?'
I dream of things that never were, and say, 'Why not?'

And more recently, Roger von Oech, president of Creative Think and a leading corporate consultant on creativity encourages all of us in the business world to break the rules and reach for the stars in his delightful *Whack on The Side of The Head:*

The worlds of thought and action overlap. What you think has a way of becoming true. If you want to be more creative, believe in the worth of your ideas, and

have the persistence to continue building on them. With this attitude, you'll take more risks, and break the rules occasionally. You'll look for more than one right answer.

Why not? Why not go for it, without hesitation and with the same Positive Mental Attitude Napoleon Hill emphasizes in *Think & Grow Rich* and so many of his other books: "Whatever the mind can conceive, it can achieve!"

Leap of faith—do what you love, do the impossible!

Every millionaire-in-training knows this, acts on it. Most truly inspiring success stories grab our attention because they inspire us to break free from our self-imposed prison and do what we are told is "impossible." Listen to how Marsha Sinetar describes the moment of her epiphany in *Do What You Love, The Money Will Follow:*

Then one day, as I drove to work along beautiful Wilshire Boulevard ... a startling thought entered my head. It was as clear a thought as if someone was speaking to me: 'Do what you love, the money will follow.' At that moment, I knew I had to, and would, take a leap of faith. I know I had to, and would, step out, cut myself loose from all those things that seemed to bind me. I knew I would start doing what I enjoyed most ...

The individual usually will not identify what he really wants because he is aiming for what he thinks is possible, rather than what he genuinely desires. Thus, he limits his goal-setting. If he wants to be a contractor, let's say, he may feel he cannot achieve that goal, and will settle for being a carpenter instead.

Again and again you will hear wise men and wise women everywhere tell you to do what you love, follow your dreams, go for it! Remember Michelangelo's bold warning: "The greatest danger for most of us is not that our aim is too high and we miss it, but that it is too low and we reach it."

Follow your bliss and you will always be rich

Nowhere has this paradox about *getting rich in spirit* as well as in fact been more powerfully expressed than by Joseph Campbell, the world's leading expert on mythology:

> **Money is congealed energy and releasing it releases life's possibilities. You realize that the possibilities of life in an economically oriented society are really a function of how much money you've got. On the other hand, money has never meant anything to me. I thought anybody who worked for money was a fool. I took a vow never to do anything for money. Now, that does not mean that when I do something I don't ask for money. I want as much as I can get, but that's the secondary part of the game.**
>
> **My life course is totally indifferent to money. As a result a lot of money has come in by doing what I feel I want to do from the inside. If you do that, you are doing things that attract money, because you are giving life and life responds in the way of its counterpart in hard coin.**
>
>> **If you follow your bliss,**
>> **you will always have your bliss,**
>> **money or not. If you follow the money,**
>> **you may lose it,**
>> **and you will have nothing.**

If you choose the path of the Zen Millionaire, you know this instinctively—you know you must follow your dreams, with passion. And you know that the key to creating wealth, to building a million dollar net worth, is to follow your bliss, whatever it may be, and do what you love. For you, there is no other way.

The Yellow Brick Road leading to the Creator Within

The money will follow at some future date. But for today, for now, in this moment, *you will know you are on the right path, because it is your path.* Joey Green put all this in a lighthearted context in the ever-charming *The Zen of Oz:*

> **The answers are within, not handed to you on a silver platter by wizard or witch. As Dorothy learns, discovering your cosmic purpose brings you home to your true nature, empowering you and your ruby slippers. And the way to discover your cosmic purpose, to achieve Oneness with your spiritual nature, is to follow the Yellow Brick Road.**

Follow *your* yellow brick road and paradoxically, once you surrender to your dreams, your journey, your destiny, success comes to your doorstep without your being obsessed about money, and without being so totally attached to tomorrow's financial rewards that they dominate your living today.

Peace of mind without an obsession for the goal

So yes, you will still go for the money. But lightly, as Cherie Carter-Scott tells us in *If Life Is A Game, These Are The Rules:*

> **If your goal is to amass a million dollars, it is natural and right for you to pursue that goal. The key to serenity, however, lies in your ability to hold lightly to the image of yourself reaching that goal. In doing so you will feel peaceful in your situation regardless of the outcome. Unattachment means you are not bound by your expectations of how things should turn out, and that you are willing to let go.**

Remember, surrender is the opposite of attachment. You live with a new mindset: Committed and focused, yet flexible and flowing with the punches. You have a goal, a million dollars net worth, at some future date. But that future goal is incidental to larger goals and does not control your daily life.

Trust that you are guided—surrender and take charge

You know that you are not alone in this venture, your higher self will guide you in creating the money—because it is already yours. Julia Cameron has a delightful way of telling us in *The Artist's Way:*

> **God has lots of money. God has lots of movie ideas, novel ideas, poems, songs, paintings, acting jobs. God has a supply of loves, friends, houses that are all available to us. By listening to the creator within, we are led to our right path. On that path we find friends, lovers, money, and meaningful work.**

With the shift in your thinking you surrender to that secret power within you, taking a cue from Zukav's incredibly trusting message in *The Seat of The Soul:*

> **Let go. Trust. Create. Be who you are ... Take your hands off the wheel. Be able to say to the Universe, 'Thy will be done,' and allow your life to go into the hands of the Universe completely. The final piece of reaching for authentic power is releasing your own to a higher form of wisdom. Release your specifications and say to the Universe: 'Find me where you know I need to be.' Let them go and trust that the Universe will provide, and so it shall. Let go of all. Let your higher self complete its task.**

You know you are not alone, you have a partner—a secret power within you that's working everywhere in your behalf, with friend and foe, near and far, now and in the future.

Whatever the mind can conceive it can achieve

This must be emphasized over and over: You are never alone. As Ernest Holmes, the founder of Science of Mind, says in *This Thing Called You:*

15

If you wish to know the truth about your business or your profession, know that it is an activity for good. It is an activity of your partnership with the Infinite. The business of life is to be happy, active and whole; to express the Divine Life with joy and in fulfillment. Lift the load of responsibility by transferring it to the Law of perfect action ... you are guided by the same Intelligence and inspired by the same Imagination which scatters the moonbeams across the waves, and holds the forces of nature in its grasp.

Bottom line: You must take full responsibility in order to fulfill your mission, to accomplish what you came here to do, the tasks you agreed to do this lifetime. And paradoxically, when you get into action, you discover you are not alone.

When you take bold actions the universe becomes your partner. You have this secret power within you—*you and the Creator are one, and together you are creating a whole new world beyond your wildest dreams, for you and for everyone.*

Every Zen Millionaire understands this fundamental principle: Your mind creates the money, not someone or something else. You do. Your mind creates the millions you envision in your dreams. Your mind is the creator. The money is already yours and flowing to you—it is already moving from universal mind, through your mind and into reality because, *whatever the mind can conceive, it will create.*

Third Secret

YOU HAVE NO COMPETITION

IN THE MILLIONAIRE'S GAME
YOU'RE PLAYING SOLITAIRE

We live in a world of scorekeepers, contests and competitions. Winners and losers. Superbowls. World champions. Olympic gold medals. Oscars. Tonys. Grammies. Golden Globes. American Idols. Top grossing. Trophies. World records. Top-10 lists, $10 million contracts, betting odds. Interest rates, capital gains, profits, losses, return on investment, the closing bell. Republicans and Democrats. Nobody really wants to be the understudy, second best, runner up.

The competition started early. Sibling rivalry. Little league. Grades and I.Q. tests. LSATs and GREs. Scholarships, MBAs and doctorates. Status symbols, the right clubs, neighborhood, friends, cars. Gucci. Guess. Polo. The right grad schools, right career path, right mentors, bosses, gurus. You are all the prizes, awards, trophies you collect. You are what you win.

Competition means winners and losers. And nobody likes being a loser. Nobody remembers the runner-up. The pressure drives many to quit, become spectators on the sidelines. But the competition continues, projecting themselves into the world. Survivors. Wheel of Fortune. Jeopardy. Lottery. Who Wants To Be A Millionaire? Whether real or fantasy, the competition continues. Status. Stars. Celebrities. Heroes. Kings and princesses. Leaders. Power. Recognition. Five minutes of fame. Or a lifetime. You live in a fiercely competitive world.

Playing a new game, by new rules—your rules

The Zen Millionaire plays a different game. If getting a million dollar net worth is part of the game you're playing, these are the new rules—and you are the only player.

You compete, but you have no competition. There is no one to beat. Only you. You're playing a game of solitaire, my friend. Which, of course, makes it easier to chase your dreams, to follow your bliss, to do what you love, because you know in your heart the money will follow. In fact, it's the only way, and you know it. Besides, you can't lose. Wayne Dyer said it best in *Real Magic:*

> **Most of us believe that money-making is a game that is played with forces outside ourselves, forces such as the economy, the stock market, interest rates, the Fed, government policies, employment statistics and the like. But as you move along a spiritual path and begin to get a taste of the power of your invisible self, you discover that money-making is merely a game that you play with yourself.**

> **Creating money is just like creating anything else in your life. It involves not being attached to it, and not giving it power over your life in any way. Authentic power does not come to you from the acquisition of money, because without the money you would then be powerless. Authentic power comes from your soul that magical place that is always within you.**

> **Money is not a goal unto itself. If you chase after it, it will always elude you.**

Of course, if you fly solo, going down your own path, the world of competition will fight you every step of the way, to keep you playing their game, by their rules.

That's right, there are enormous risks in being unconventional, contrarian, different, unique, radical, the oddball. Yes, the rewards are great. But the path is littered with wounded losers. And along the way, something called "reality" sets in. Very few make it from the sandlots to the pros. Most people avoid the battering, stay protected by the herd, never straying too far. Spectators.

You break the rules, and you make the rules

But what if you are playing a game of solitaire? It takes great courage to follow your dreams, a willingness to confront the system and break the rules. To stand up when an authority traps you with an impossible challenge, an obvious no-win scenario. And retort, as the young Capt. James T. Kirk did in this scene in *Star Trek, The Kobayashi Maru:*

> **"The no-win scenario is the basis of our universe," Constrev replied. "That's garbage," Kirk interrupted, "I don't have to play by the rules. I don't believe in the no-win scenario."**

Get it! If you want to be a Zen Millionaire you are going down a road less traveled, you will have to break the conventional rules and risk rejection by the many people around you. But you have no choice. You are the one Henry David Thoreau had in mind when he wrote:

> **If a man does not keep pace with his companions, perhaps it is because he hears a different drummer. Let him step to the music which he hears, however measured and far away.**

In reality, of course, nobody has any competition out there. *Nobody.* And you can withdraw from the competition any time. But that's not the path of the Zen Millionaire. Rather, paradoxically, *you stay in the game.* You compete, but you play by the rules you make up, rules that fit who you are. Or by breaking the rules of their game. Your choice. Not theirs.

19

You are totally responsible—no one to blame

Win or lose, either way, you're stuck with the results. You are responsible, totally and absolutely. You get the trophy if you win. And if you lose, you have no one to blame.

Yes, most people do whine and point fingers, blame others. You can't. It doesn't work. No matter what, you're stuck with the results. You and you alone are responsible. Period. Wall Street money manager Jack Schwager was very blunt about this in *The New Market Wizards:*

> **Whether you win or lose, you are responsible for your own results. Even if you lost on your broker's tip, an advisory service recommendation, or a bad signal from the system you bought, you are responsible, because you made the decision to listen and act... Do your own thinking. Don't get caught up in mass hysteria. By the time a story is making the covers of the national periodicals, the trend is probably near the end. Never listen to the opinions of others.**

You want to be a Zen Millionaire? Don't give away your power, ever! Take responsibility, regardless of the results. You're it! Stay centered and play your game, by your rules. The competitor-with-no-competition often gets their cues from the great contrarians, icons like Oscar-winning Clint Eastwood:

> **Anytime anybody tells me that the trend is such and such, I do the opposite. I got where I am by coming off the wall.**

If you're a Zen Millionaire, you're coming off the wall, your wall. Marching to a different drummer. You know you're on a solo trip. Playing a game of solitary. You compete, but you know you have no competition.

This is a classic koan, one of those mind games played by the great Zen masters, a contradiction in terms, an impossible challenge with impossible rules that you break and win anyway. All great athletes know they are competing against themselves, rising to new levels of excellence, daily pushing the envelope to reach yet another new personal best. And jazz great Branford Marsalis' message is exactly the same:

> **I don't care who likes it or buys it. Because if you use that criteria, Mozart would have never written Don Giovanni, Charlie Parker would never have played anything but swing music. There comes a point at which you have to stand up and say, this is what I have to do.**

The Zen Millionaire is playing the money game by the same rules, their own rules, in a game where there is no competition.

Trust the still small voice within you

Financial expert Suze Orman put this same message in the context of the competitive world of money in *The 9 Steps to Financial Freedom:*

> **Whether you want to believe it or not—you and you alone have the best judgment when it comes to your money. You must do what makes you feel safe, sound, comfortable. You must trust yourself more than you trust others, and that inner voice will tell you when it is time to take action.**

Get it! Trust yourself. The money game is a game of solitaire. You are a competitor with no competition. Only you. No one to blame. The results are all yours, win or lose. And if you play by "their" rules, you will lose. Zen Millionaires play by their own rules. Know when to break the rules. Know that "money-making is merely a game that you play with yourself."

PART TWO

ZEN DISCIPLINE
and the
MILLIONAIRE-IN-TRAINING

Why become a millionaire: Freedom to do what you love? Actually, it's the other way around. Your best chance of becoming a millionaire is by doing what you love, today, not waiting until you retire—just ask any millionaire-next-door. If you love what you're doing, you're more efficient, more focused, more productive. Most people don't get it. They just hope 'something' will magically happen, but wishful thinking rarely works. You need disciplined action.

The truth is, most of us aren't saving enough today to retire tomorrow. Our savings rate is at a historic low. We are spending too much and saving only about a third of what's necessary for retirement. The net worth of the typical American family is only $15,000, exclusive of home equity. Consumers are caught up in a commercial world that relentlessly drives us to spend, buy, accumulate stuff.

We want a quick fix, to get all we can, as fast as we can, parading our possessions for everybody to see. But for two-thirds of Americans, the hope of retiring is wishful thinking. In fact, half of the people over 65 would be living in poverty if not for their meager Social Security check. Saving and investing for the future are no longer part of our nation's values as they once were.

So anyone who is serious about planning for the future, while enjoying today, must take contrary actions, make a dramatic shift in behavior and start living with a new mindset, usually in direct conflict with their community, their culture and the conventional wisdom. Long before you become a millionaire you must adopt the tough discipline of a millionaire-in-training.

Fourth Secret

YOU ARE MASTER
OF THE GAME ... AND ALWAYS A
BEGINNER

Yes, you are master of the money game. You have all you need to win. Your power comes not from any guru, expert, leader, superior or any other kind of authority. Not from any outside authorities. "Conservative money management isn't hard. Be your own guru," says Jane Bryant Quinn in her personal finance best-seller, *Making The Most of Your Money.* Your power comes from your "beginner's mind." From ancient times, all masters have lived with this strange paradox, where the master is a student, a beginner, a servant. Shunryu Suzuki describes this simple principle in his classic, *Zen Mind, Beginner's Mind:*

> **Our 'original mind' includes everything within itself. It is always rich and *sufficient within itself.* You should not lose your self-sufficient state of mind. This does not mean a closed mind, but actually an empty mind and a ready mind. If your mind is empty, it is always ready for anything; it is open to everything. In the beginner's mind there are many possibilities, in the expert's mind there are few.**

You stop relying on experts. Trust your instincts, do it yourself—use your beginner's mind. We hear the same message from one of the most successful money managers of all time, Fidelity Magellan's legendary Peter Lynch writing in *One Up On Wall Street:*

> **Think like an amateur. If you invest like an institution, you're doomed to perform like one, which in most cases isn't very well. If you're a surfer, a truck driver, a high school dropout, or an eccentric retiree, then you've got an edge already.**

Your world is a moving target. Just when you think you got it figured out, mastered, somebody will move it again. A beginner's mind is the single best tool you have in finding solutions to the constant flow of new challenges, when old rules-of-thumb, last week's data and outdated strategies stop working.

Not yet there ... keep climbing, farther up

This principle is also a great way for keeping your ego in check. Philip Toshio Sudo talks about all this in his delightful little book, *Zen Guitar:*

> **The first rule of mastery is this: Those who think themselves masters are not masters. There can be no let-up of your study, no matter how far you've come. Even the highest priests of Zen say so to themselves, *mi zai:* 'Not yet.' You have not yet learned all you can know. You have not yet given all you can give. You have not yet reached the summit. Empty your cup and keep going. Same mountain, farther up.**

Here's another powerful voice echoing the same principle. Aikido master and *Look* magazine editor George Leonard encourages you to shift your gaze, off the destination and back to the journey, away from the goals, whether you are chasing mastery, enlightenment, a gold medal, or a million dollars net worth:

> **What is Mastery? It resists definition yet can be instantly recognized. It comes in many varieties, yet follows certain unchanging laws. It brings rich rewards, yet is**

not really a goal or a destination but rather a process, a journey.

We call this journey *mastery,* and tend to assume that it requires a special ticket available only to those born with special abilities. But mastery isn't reserved for the super-talented or even for those who are fortunate enough to have gotten an early start. It is available to everyone who is willing to get on the path and stay on it … Mastery is not perfection, but rather a journey, and the true master must be willing to try and fail and try again.

Leonard also turns the concept of mastery on its head telling us not only that true mastery is the original mind of the eternal student, but the ability to go further, take risks, make mistakes, even if it means looking foolish at times:

It's simple. To be a learner, you've got to be willing to be a fool … I began to see more than a casual relationship between learning and the willingness to be foolish, between master and fool, to be clear, I don't mean stupid, but one with the spirit of the medieval fool, the court jester, the carefree fool in the Tarot deck who bears the awesome number zero, signifying the fertile void from which all creation springs, the state of emptiness that allows new things to come into being.

If you are on this path, by now you are a living example of this very real contradiction—between the Zen master's vow of poverty and the millionaire-in-training's goal of creating create wealth.

If it is true, as so many masters say, Zen has nothing to teach, if you already have all you need to know within you to be an enlightened Buddha and a Zen master, and if you have all that is necessary to compete successfully in the financial world—then why the concern about being beginner? Sounds like a step backward doesn't it, a bit of reverse ego?

In the mind of the master, you are "never ahead"

Actually there is no contradiction, no paradox, no koan. You know Zen masters cannot *give* you anything, cannot *teach* you anything. Yet, as Joe Hyams says in *Zen and The Martial Arts,* "even masters have masters."

Of course Zen has nothing to teach. But *you* have much Zen to learn. Much experience to attain. Much life to live. A million steps to take. And a lifetime to learn, as your life becomes "one damn thing after another," as Mark Twain once said about everyday life.

Sports superstars grasp this reality of the beginner's mind from yet another angle. Listen to how the famous money manager Mark McCormack described it in his highly practical *What They Don't Teach You at Harvard Business School:*

The champion's true edge exists solely in the mind, and over the years I have observed three attitudinal characteristics which are common to every superstar I have ever known ... dissatisfaction with their own accomplishments. They use any success, any victory, as a spur to greater ambition ... an ability to peak their performance, to get themselves up for major tournaments and events ... and ability to psych out their opponent. This is referred to as 'the killer instinct' but that tells you more about the result than what is going on mentally. In the champion's mind he is never ahead.

The Zen Millionaire will play the money game with the attitude of a champion in a sporting contest. But the game is incidental, you are playing to achieve mastery of yourself. And yet you are always approaching the world with the freshness, the newness, the awareness of a youthful beginner's mind.

In matters of investing, personal finance, retirement planning and other money matters, you are always the master with total responsibility, and at the same time, always a beginner willing to step in asking foolish questions in order to be a champion, always at the top of your game. Easy to say, not always easy to do, says Suzuki:

The most difficult thing is always to keep a beginner's mind. There is no need for a deep understanding of Zen ... appreciate your beginner's mind. It is the secret of Zen practice.

Honor that secret: Mastery as a Zen Millionaire means you are a perpetual beginner, with money, family, business associates, everywhere in your world.

THE MASTERMIND IS
CENTERED
WITHIN YOU
TRUST IT

The mind of the Zen Millionaire is centered within—all day, every day. You do not rely on gurus, bosses, experts and outside authorities to tell you what to do, make your decisions, run your life. Listen with an open mind, but trust yourself. No one will do it for you. In his book, *Don't Worry, Make Money,* psychologist Richard Carlson warns us against falling into this trap:

> **A major mistake made by many is to give away one's power to perceived experts. We do it all the time—to our doctors, financial planners, insurance salesmen. Always remember, if you're going to make money, you must take charge. Abundance and joy come from within you, not from other people.**

If you are going to make money, there is only one way to do it—you must take charge. And when you do, the center of the world will shift back to where it always has been—within you, in alignment with the universe. The Zen Millionaire knows the 'kingdom of heaven' is within. Knows the secret power is within. The universe is centered within you, and you are one with it. Martial arts champion Chuck Norris describes this balanced center in simple language:

The Zen masters believe that the way of the universe is a way of remaining in balance and in harmony with nature. Moving with and not against energy can open the creative paths of the mind. You will then be at one with the universe. In the truest Zen sense, you will be the center of the universe, no matter where you are or the circumstances you find yourself in. This source of inner power, called *Ki,* is an invisible life force that flows throughout the universe ... By being 'centered'— being focused and in touch with that 'one point'—we can make use of this universal energy.

Being centered within yourself and in sync with the power of the universe is the key to success. There are no higher authorities "out there," no broker, adviser, securities analyst, or fund manager can do it for you—no one, *not even a great spiritual master.* Trust no one says Alan Watts one of the greatest popularizers of Zen in America:

I am not a guru, in the sense of a spiritual teacher or authority from which you may expect something more than you have. When you confer spiritual authority to another person, you must realize you are allowing them to pick your pocket and sell you your own watch.

If you decide to be a millionaire in spirit and in fact, then *you must sit in the center of the financial universe.* However, *staying* centered is not an easy task because we are our own worst enemy, as money manager Martin Pring warned his professional colleagues in *The Psychology of Investing Explained:*

For most of us, the task of beating the markets is not difficult, it is the job of beating ourselves that proves to be overwhelming ... mastering our emotions and attempting to think independently, as well as not being swayed by those around us.

If staying centered is difficult for full-time investment professionals, it is far more problematic for the average investor on Main Street

America. Why? Because ego and emotions, fear and greed, over-optimism, preconceptions and ideologies will constantly sabotage your decision-making abilities.

Centered within—the power of the universe

There are impostors, saboteurs, inner ninjas, distracting us from our source, and as such no different from external distractions. Making us feel guided rather than distracted, invincible rather than confused. The Zen Millionaire sees the deception, following the advice of money manager Jack Schwager in *The New Market Wizards:*

> **You need to do your own thinking … Whether you win or lose, you are responsible for your own results. Even if you lost on your broker's tip, an advisory service recommendation, or a bad signal from the system you bought, you are responsible, because you made the decision to listen and act … Never listen to the opinions of others … Do your own thinking.**

This centering principle goes beyond money issues, into the core of your soul, permeating your entire life. In *Instructions to the Cook: A Zen Master's Lessons in Living a Life That Matters,* Bernard Glassman and Rick Fields put this principle in an action-oriented context:

> **Suppose you don't have any money, but you have an idea of something you want to create. But if you sit around in your backyard and say, 'I can't do anything because I have no money,' who's going to join you? If you say, 'Let's do something,' you'll get joined by thousands of people from all over. People are attracted to action. People want to see that idea realized, as a book or new kind of cookie or any product, for that matter, and money will come to it.**

We hear the same message over and over from many corners of our world: Oscar winner Anthony Hopkins says "be bold, and mighty forces will come to your aid." Ralph Waldo Emerson put it this way:

"The world makes way for a man who knows where he is going." Conversely, you will not attract money unless you are centered. Why? Because you don't know where you are going.

Trust your inner voices, and act on them

If you don't know where you are going, or where you've been, or where you are right now—you are adrift. Out of touch with your power source. You are off-center. Easy prey. Vulnerable to being controlled by others. Money will elude you.

The Zen Millionaire instinctively understands this reality, stays focused and centered, aligning—*or rather constantly realigning*—with this Higher Power. When it comes to money issues, you must stay centered and trust your inner voice as completely as Wayne Dyer does in *Real Magic:*

> **Develop a trust in your intuitive voices … If you feel a strong inner inclination to change jobs, or locations, or to be around new people, or to try a particular investment, then place more trust in that hunch. This is your divine guidance encouraging you to take a risk, to ignore the ways of the herd, to be the unique individual that you are. Prosperity will be your experience in life, if that is how you begin to process life inside. It is the inside that counts the most …**

> **My hunches have always guided my investments. I can honestly say that the only time I experienced a big loss financially was when I ignored my intuition … You can be spiritual and have nice things. You can be spiritual and have money flow into your life.**

With practice, the Zen Millionaire discovers that the centered way of life not only works, it is the only way to live with peace of mind.

If you hesitate at this point, know you are in good company. Napoleon Hill eventually learned that at the center of the *Secrets of Success* he got from the billionaire Andrew Carnegie was a power that came through all millionaires in his Mastermind group of five hundred business and financial leaders:

> **The Master Mind: An alliance of two or more minds blended in a spirit of perfect harmony and co-operating for the attainment of a single purpose ... For many years I was so sensitive concerning the unseen Guides, whose presence I had felt, that I carefully avoided all references to them, in both my writings and public lectures. Then one day ... I began to make inquiries of the hundreds of successful men who collaborated with me in the organization of the Science of Success, and discovered that *each of them* had received guidance from unknown sources.**

On one hand this reticence to talk about mysterious guides is based on a fear of seeming overly-zealous to other people. On a deeper level, however, it reflects the ancient Taoist wisdom: "Those who know do not speak, those who speak do not know." After all, if you really are centered in this secret power within, there is no need to talk about it, you just trust it, and get into action.

Trust you are guided by a universal mastermind

The Zen Millionaire will have a similar reluctance to discuss any mysterious mastermind guidance system. You know it is never "out there," it is at once within you and it is also universal, available to everyone, everywhere, anytime, for the asking. But it is tough to explain, so often best left unsaid. So quietly go within, listen and trust it, in the simple way suggested by Warren Buffett, one of the great Zen Millionaires:

> **A great IQ is not needed to do well as an investor. Just the ability to detach yourself from the crowd.**

Detach from the crowd and center your mind within, all day, every day. A mysterious mastermind is guiding you. Get to know it intimately and trust it implicitly. There are no external authorities who know better than you what's best for you. None. Carl Jung says you are at the center of all life:

The great events of the world are, at bottom, profoundly unimportant. In the last analysis, the essential thing is the life of the individual, here alone do the great transformations take place, and the whole future, the whole history of the world, ultimately springs as a gigantic summation from these hidden resources in individuals.

Take full command of your life, if you are a Zen Millionaire you know the Mastermind is centered with you, and you are one with the universe. Know it, believe it, trust it, for you are rich in spirit and in fact. That is the secret of success.

Sixth Secret

BEING ENLIGHTENED IS
"NOTHING SPECIAL"
NEITHER IS BEING
A MILLIONAIRE

From ancient time Zen masters have reminded students that being enlightened is "nothing special." And today, we learn that neither is being a millionaire "special." Just ask any one of the "millionaires next door" that Thomas Stanley writes about: They look and act just like the rest of the folks in the neighborhood. Joe Hyams captured this phenomenon in this wonderful little story from his classic *Zen and The Martial Arts:*

One day it was announced by Master Joshu that the young monk Kyogen had reached an enlightened state. Much impressed by the news, several of his peers went to speak with him. 'We have heard that you are enlightened. Is this true?' his fellows inquired? 'It is,' Kyogen answered. 'Tell us,' said a friend, 'how do you feel?' 'As miserable as ever,' replied the enlightened Kyogen.

A million dollars can buy you a better house or car, but otherwise money alone changes very little, and may even make things more difficult for you, if you don't get the Zen first. Professor Jacob Needleman, author of *Money & the Meaning of Life,* brought home this point in *Fast Company* magazine:

Money makes us unjustifiably feel that we're better and more important than we really are. When money

can make us feel humble, then I think it's really useful. ... If you are worrying about vegetables now, you'll be worrying about yachts then. You're a worrier. It's in you, not the money. Life is not much defined by the external situation as by the inner one. Having money won't change your internal makeup. If you're an anxious sob without money, you're going to be an anxious sob with a lot of money.

The solution? The old masters offered this familiar advice to the newly enlightened: "Before enlightenment, you chop wood, you carry water. After enlightenment, you chop wood, you carry water." A Zen Millionaire might well paraphrase that simple bit of advice:

Before you are a millionaire, you worked hard, saved regularly each month, invested wisely. After you're a millionaire, you work hard, save regularly each month, invest wisely.

You shop for groceries, go to the gym, order a Big Mac, nurse colds, take out the garbage, put your pants on one leg at a time, pay more bills. You still "chop wood, carry water." Same old stuff. Not much changes. Most millionaires just do not buy extravagant toys, collectibles, antique cars and yachts. You don't read about them in *People* and *Fortune*. They are inconspicuous average folks. Being a millionaire, like being enlightened, really is "nothing special."

Buffett's trillion dollar barbecue

You may recall that ancient bit of wisdom from Lao Tzu's 5,000-year-old *Tao Te Ching:* "Those who know do not speak, those who speak do not know." A multi-millionaire attending Warren Buffett's annual barbecue in Omaha, Nebraska a few years ago sounded every bit like a Zen master par excellence in an email he sent to me:

The 'Millionaire Next Door' missed what I call the 'Berkshire Hathaway' effect. I don't know if you have ever been to Warren's party in Omaha, but this year over one trillion dollars in net worth walked in the door.

Many of these people attend Warren's party as a form of entertainment, like going to a family reunion. For example, my family first bought five shares of Berkshire Hathaway in 1968 at $22 a share as a joke. That 'joke' has turned into $400 thousand, and that's one of our smaller investments.

Most people with money ain't talking, but are well taken care of. They don't drive flashy cars or live in big houses, but they're very comfortable. And they don't need a six figure income to survive. They live very comfortably on $15,000 to $30,000 a year and still save lots of money. And a lot of their wealth doesn't show up in surveys. Undeveloped land, child's life insurance policies, all kinds of collectibles, foreign bank accounts, etc. Their 'biggest problem' is how to give away their wealth!

Nothing special. Most millionaires live rather normal lives without flaunting their wealth. Normal? More accurately, they're "boring!" They are not wasting money buying from the *Robb Report* and *Opulence* magazines. They're frugal masters, shopping for deals at Wal-Mart. Seriously, listen to how Charles Carlson summarizes this simple truth in *Eight $teps to $even Figures:*

Millionaire investors, by society's standards, are boring people ... They don't job hop. They marry once ... They stay in the same house for long stretches of time. They buy and hold the same investments for five years or more. Boring right? Yes, the typical millionaire investor's life may lack a certain variety. But variety, while perhaps the spice of life, is poison to building wealth ... consistency builds wealth.

Remember, being rich is nothing special for the eight million American millionaires. For many, their biggest problem may be giving it all away. But their greatest challenge is: *Making their money and their lives mean something.* The money is nothing special. Yet very special. Life is a gift. So is a million bucks. Be grateful. Act responsibly. Give of your gifts, quietly.

What about the thirty million American millionaires-in-training, those who don't have the net worth yet, but are working on it? Still "nothing special."

Nothing special—not enlightenment, not a million bucks

Same with a Zen Millionaire. You get the money—*and even the Zen, even the spirituality*—it's still nothing special. If it is, watch out, your ego's taking over.

Some years ago a business executive I was interviewing for a documentary on transformation put this in sharp focus. If your ego is inflated, telling you that you are different, that you really do have something special, that you are enlightened, or famous, or a successful millionaire, be careful! He was laughing as he explained:

> **If you think you've got 'it,' and you think that you're better than the guy next door, then you ain't got 'it!'**

Do *you* get it? The ancient masters call this the "stink of Zen," another not-so-subtle way of saying that if you do think being a Zen Millionaire is something special, you ain't got the "Zen first" yet! Diana and Richard Saint Ruth put it quite simply:

> **When Zen followers become proud of their achievements or have delusions about their practices, that is sometimes called 'the stink of Zen.' It means that they are showing off, concerned about appearances and acquiring affectations. This is being a Zen fraud. It is easy to learn Zen-speak, a way of talking that does not mean anything but can impress those who do not know any better. It is also easy to justify crazy behavior by calling it 'Zen, the spontaneous way of living.' This is the 'stink' of Zen.**

Similarly, Alan Watts' description of Zen spirituality sounds remarkably similar to the way Stanley talks about millionaires:

In studying or practicing Zen it is of no help to think about Zen. To remain caught up in ideas and words about Zen is, as the old masters say, to 'stink of Zen.' For this reason the masters talk of Zen as little as possible, and throw concrete reality straight at us.

Get it! Nothing special. Not enlightenment. Not a million bucks. Not being a millionaire. Not a millionaire-in-training. Not even being a Zen Millionaire. *Even this Zen spirituality is nothing special.* Period.

Unfortunately, our egos have a way of telling us we're different. Telling us that this Zen Millionaire status is something 'more special' than being 'nothing special.' Folks, it is not. You are not. That's a dangerous mental trap. "If you think you are better than the next guy, you ain't got it," you are certainly not enlightened. Not a Zen Millionaire. You may be a millionaire, but you have the stink of Zen. You don't get it.

You may also be one—*and not know it, or care!*

A Zen Millionaire may know all this instinctively, quietly, deep within, without making a big fuss about it, to himself or others. Why? Because it really is no big deal. Nobody has ever described it better than Veronique Vienne in her works, *The Art of Doing Nothing* and *The Art of Imperfection:*

What is enlightenment? …. Hundreds of Zen stories tell of how monks failed to attain satori after decades of practice, only to stumble on it by accident. The anecdotes are interpreted as evidence that you can only prepare for spiritual change, you cannot control it. Reaching enlightenment is a bit like winning the lottery—not a million-dollar bonanza, mind you, just fifty bucks … Your moment of enlightenment came packaged as a thought bubble. On a scale of one to ten, it was probably a number four insight...

Enlightenment is just another word for feeling comfortable with being a completely ordinary person.

At long last, the unexceptional seems extraordinary enough: a puddle of water, a child running after a bird, the peaceful hum of your computer—and you, in the midst of it all, with your unvarnished self-image. The charade is over and a painful existential headache is gone. You are not a perfect human being—far from it— but your mind is clear.

Ten good reasons to be an ordinary person ... #10. You are enlightened, though you don't know what it means ... let alone care about it.

And here's one final bit of advice to tuck away for future reference when you do have that million bucks, and you are rich in spirit and in fact. Zen master Suzuki reminds us in his ever-gentle way that "there are, strictly speaking, no enlightened people, there is only enlightened activity." The past is a rapidly fading memory, the future is at best a dream. But the present is here, it is now, and you must seize it with all your might, for enlightenment only exists in the present moment.

PART THREE

EARLY RETIREMENT
HEAVEN ON EARTH
nirvana
RETIRE YOUNG
RETIRE RICH
RETIRE HAPPY
RETIRE NOW

"Early retirement" is more than a metaphor, it is a new state of mind, an inner sense of freedom—*today, not tomorrow!* Most Americans work for thirty years or more controlled by large impersonal companies imprisoned in jobs that drain their spirit. For them, retirement is the dream of a distant future when they may be financially independent.

Financial freedom is their ultimate goal. A time when they can finally to do what they love, when they can express who they really are—creating, traveling, volunteering, visiting family, a favorite hobby, or that career or business you always dreamed about—without the worries of having to work for enough money to survive the daily struggles of the competitive, commercial jungle that has become the American way of life.

The sense of financial freedom is not a dream, is never in the future. You must live it today, now. The smart ones aren't just planning to save enough to retire someday in the distant future—they are determined to get "enough" to retire early and finally do what they love.

But the smartest, the Zen Millionaires, are already "retired," they are at peace within themselves, in harmony with their world, they already have enough, now, today. They already have financial freedom, they know it deep in the mind, body, soul and spirit. They are free. They are rich in spirit and in fact. When they get the million bucks, it will be "nothing special," as the Zen masters say about the goal of enlightenment. Money will change nothing for the Zen Millionaire, because they already have all they need.

WEALTH-BUILDING
IS ALL ABOUT
CHARACTER
BUILDING

The purpose of money and wealth-creation is character building—every day, through opportunities, challenges and choices, decisions, discipline, integrity and our actions. With every dime and dollar we spend, save, give, invest. In *Money & the Meaning of Life* the philosopher Jacob Needleman tells us how character is the true measure of our success in life:

> **In Yiddish there are about a 1,000 words that mean "fool." There's only one word that means an authentic human being: 'Mensch.' My grandmother would say 'You've got to be a Mensch,' and that has to do with what we used to call character. To be successful means to have character …**

> **We philosophers can't really figure this out better than anyone else. And money won't buy you an answer. Only worldly experience with lots of adventures and making lots of money may finally let you come away from it saying, 'There's something money can't buy. I can't put my finger on it, but I sense it.'**

Very Zen, you are thrown back on your own experience—and your conscience, the still small voice, the secret power within—not the second-hand experience of some guru, priest or pundit.

The founder of Templeton Funds, Sir John Marks Templeton, is someone who has made a lot of money, while at the same time dedicating his life and his fortune to character-building as well as wealth-building. Here's a note on character, conscience and the spirit from his book, *Worldwide Laws of Life:*

> **Thomas MacCaullay says that 'the measure of a man's real character is what he would do if he would never be found out.' Would he be totally honest and above board with others? Would he cheat or steal? If what is done in secret stays a secret, what would you do? How would you live? If you found a wallet stuffed with money, would you return it to the owner?**
>
> **Our conscience can often be our friend and our guide. It nudges us when we contemplate doing something wrong. It warns us of the danger that could be done to us or others. It is important to listen to that inner voice. The person who learns or chooses to ignore his conscience often forsakes his best friend and lifetime guide.**
>
> **If the measure of a person's real character is determined by what he would do if he weren't found out, the only person capable of judging his actions is the person himself and God.**

Which sounds remarkably similar to a statement made before the United States Congress by one of America's richest men. Warren Buffett was crystal clear about how much more important character is than money. He confronts his staff with a blunt warning that should force anyone to dig deep into their conscience—that still small voice—for guidance:

> **I want employees to ask themselves whether they are willing to have any contemplated act appear on the front page of their local paper the next day ... If they follow this test, they will not fear my other message to them: Lose money for my firm and I will be understanding; lose a shred of reputation for the firm, and I will be ruthless.**

If you listen closely to these men, you see how character embodies many intangibles: Integrity. Values. Morals. Ethics. Principles. Character-building is essential to the success of the Zen Millionaire.

Stephen Covey is another mentor who has dedicated his life to character-building. Covey separates the "Character Ethic," which guided Ben Franklin and America's founding fathers, from the "Personality Ethic." In *The Seven Habits of Highly-Effective People, Restoring the Character Ethic*, Covey describes these two ethical ways of living:

> **The Character Ethic** **is based on the fundamental idea that there are principles that govern human effectiveness— natural laws in the human dimension that are just as real, just as unchanging and unarguably 'there' as laws such as gravity are in the physical dimension ... natural laws that cannot be broken.**

> **The Personality Ethic. Success is a function of personality, of public image, of attitudes and behaviors, skills and techniques, that lubricate the processes of interaction.**

Character-building, an "unchanging natural law that cannot be broken," is also a core principle of the Zen Millionaires. Character-building is the basis of all wealth-building. In *Principle-Centered Leadership,* Covey details the three key elements in the Character Ethic:

> **Integrity. I define integrity as the value we place on ourselves. As we clearly identify our values and proactively organize and execute around our priorities on a daily basis, we develop self-awareness and self-value by making and keeping meaningful promises and commitments ...**

> **Maturity. I define maturity as the balance between courage and consideration. If a person can express his feelings and convictions with courage balanced with**

consideration for the feelings for another person, he is mature ...

Abundance Mentality. **Our thinking is that there is plenty out there for everybody. Abundance mentality flows out of a deep sense of personal worth and security. It results in sharing recognition, profits, and responsibility. It opens new options and alternatives. It turns personal joy and fulfillment outward. It recognizes unlimited possibilities for positive interaction, growth, and development.**

A character rich in integrity, maturity, and the abundance mentality has a genuineness that goes far beyond technique. Your character is constantly radiating, communicating. From it, people come to trust or distrust you.

Know this: The purpose of money in the hands of a Zen Millionaire is character building—through opportunities, challenges and discipline learned in life experiences, for as philosopher James Allen said: "Circumstances do not make a man, they reveal him."

Figure out what's "right," then do it!

In short, the most revealing crisis in your journey to becoming a millionaire will be a simple question you must ask yourself every day: Are you building character on the way to creating wealth? Are you getting rich in spirit and in fact?

If you are a millionaire-in-training, living in the spirit of Zen, your path demands a life of integrity, maturity and a mindset of abundance. There is no halfway with character. You either get it or you don't. You live it or you don't. As Harold Kushner says in *Living a Life That Matters,* in order to build character, you must make doing what's right your soul priority:

Integrity means being whole, unbroken, undivided. It describes a person who has united the different parts of his or her personality, so that there is no

longer a split in the soul. When your soul is divided, part of you wants to do one thing while part wants to something else, you are at war with yourself …

When you have integrity, all of your aspirations are focused in one direction. Like the karate expert who can break a board with his bare hand by focusing all his strength on one spot, the person of integrity, the person whose soul is not fragmented, can do great things by concentrating all of his energies on a single goal. For the person of integrity, life may not be easy but it is simple: Figure out what is right and do it. All other considerations come in second."

So the path of the Zen Millionaire is not a choice between building a million dollar net worth and building character, they go hand-in-hand. The truth is that if you want to build character, you must want it with the same determination as a new student of Zen wants their training. A story from Chuck Norris' *The Secret Power Within* makes this point:

The truth is that getting into Zen can be hard, if not absolutely impossible, if you go at it the wrong way. If you presented yourself at the door of a Zen monastery in Japan and requested instruction in Zen, you'd be turned away … This refusal at the door is part of the tradition. In fact it is the first lesson of Zen and is designed to turn away everyone except the truly dedicated….

That is why it's easier to follow the "rules" of Wall Street and Corporate America and get rich in fact—and never get rich in spirit, never let money help you build character.

If you waver or doubt, you're sure to fail. And what could be a better imitation of life than finding yourself faced with the responsibility for performing a series of chores, things you've never done before, without advance warning, without prior instruction, and without guidance or help? And sometimes in life you find yourself alone and ignored in the rain.

How important is your character, your values, your integrity, your principles? When faced with a choice—between cash and conscience—are you willing to put character building ahead of building your net worth? Are you willing to stand alone in the rain to do what's right, every day for the rest of your life f necessary? At the moment of truth—*if your story ever does make the front pages of your local newspaper*—will you be revealed as a person of character, of integrity, of principles, rich in fact and in spirit?

Eighth Secret

MAKE PEACE
WITH
THE DARKSIDE
AND "BLESS THE DARKNESS
AS YOU BLESS THE LIGHT"

In a *Fast Company* magazine interview, the philosopher and teacher, Jacob Needleman, author of *Money & the Meaning of Life,* put this challenge of the darkside in an ancient historical, as well as a psychological struggle that you, me and everyone must confront, it is part of all life:

In our time and culture, the battlefield of life is money. Instead of horses and chariots, guns and fortresses, there are banks, checkbooks, credit cards, mortgages, salaries, the IRS. But the inner enemies remain the same now as they were in ancient India or feudal Japan: fear, self-deception, vanity, egoism, wishful thinking, tension, and violence ... enemies of inner development, enemies which one cannot hide from in overly protective monasteries.

This scenario is unavoidable, you are unprotected in the combative worlds of Wall Street and Corporate America. And yet, paradoxically, if you want to be a millionaire in spirit as well as in fact, the darkside can be transformed into your greatest ally on the journey.

Dalai Lama—you must face the darkside

Or your greatest enemy—the saboteur, the inner ninja—draining your power, undermining the 'secret power within you.' Either way the Zen Millionaire has no choice but to confront the darkside, for as the Dalai Lama warns you in *Ethics for the New Millennium:*

> **If we try to avoid or deny a given problem by simply ignoring it or taking to drink or drugs, or even some forms of meditation or prayer as a means of escape, while there is a chance of short-term relief, the problem itself remains.**

Facing the darkside is not easy, especially since it is hidden in our denial. And yet we truly have no choice. In many of his works the psychologist Carl G. Jung warns us to deal with this relentless challenge from the shadowy depths, for it will never go away and will forever remain a hidden minefield sabotaging us on the road to becoming a millionaire:

> **The most terrifying thing is to accept oneself completely ... One does not become enlightened by imagining figures of light but by making the darkness conscious ... He is no hero who has never met the dragon ... only one who has risked the fight with the dragon and is not overcome by it wins ... He alone has a claim to self-confidence, for he has faced the dark ground of his self and thereby gained himself ... *A whole person is one who has walked with God and wrestled with the devil.***

Who is this "whole person" you are searching for? Writing in *The Prophet,* the philosopher poet Kahlil Gibran describes the whole person as the person at peace with themselves who will "bless the darkness as you bless the light." Unfortunately, we discover early in life that the path to wholeness is neither easy, nor swift, nor fun—a fact that drives so many to gurus, confessors and psychologists, in hopes of finding the missing wealth, peace and happiness.

Buddha's Four Nobles—exposing our secrets

Of course the big problem for so many of us is that we don't know we have a problem. We are in denial. We project our darkside on people, things and events "out there." Yes, we have a secret, but we keep the secret hidden within us, *even from ourselves.* Unlocking that secret is the central focus of Jungian therapy. As he put it, the secret is:

> **A story that is not told, and which as a rule no one knows of. It is the patient's secret, the rock against which he is shattered. If I knew his secret story I have a key to the treatment ... the problem is always the whole person, never the symptoms alone.**

The same idea underlies Zen training. In his book, the *Four Noble Truths,* the Dalai Lama tells us these truths arise from *duhkha,* suffering. Not physical pain but suffering deep in the psyche and soul, what we also see as the stress and anxieties, struggles and frustrations of everyday life. In *The Road Less Traveled,* psychiatrist M. Scott Peck puts this ancient teaching in a modern context, beginning with this simple summary of Buddha's Four Noble Truths:

> **Life is difficult. This is a great truth, one of the greatest truths. It is a great truth because once we see the truth, we transcend it. Once we truly know that life is difficult— once we truly understand and accept it—-then life is no longer difficult. Because once it is accepted, the fact that life is difficult no longer matters.**
>
> **Most do not fully see that life is difficult. Instead they moan more or less incessantly, noisily or subtly, about their problems, their burdens, and their difficulties as if life were generally easy, as if life *should* be easy. Life is a series of problems. Do we want to moan about them or solve them?**
>
> **What makes life difficult is that the process of confronting and solving problems is a painful one ...**

Wise people learn not to dread but actually to welcome problems and actually to welcome the pain of problems. Most of us are not so wise. Facing the pain involved, almost all of us, to a greater of lesser degree, attempt to avoid problems ... We attempt to get out of them rather than suffer through them.

Now let's put this in context for the millionaire-in-training. Investment adviser and psychiatrist, John Schott, author of *Mind Over Money,* described this darkside challenge in concrete financial behavior in *Psychology Today:*

Investing is a simple matter: Buy good stocks and hold on to them, and time will make you rich. This is the most common bit of advice given to beginning investors. But if it's true that investing is so simple, then why do people wind up losing money on stocks, view the market as a major gamble, or feel too intimidated to invest in the first place?

Because every emotional drive associated with money gets played out in investing: The longing for security, the guilt engendered by greed, the quest for power and self-esteem, the fear of being abandoned, the search for love, the dream of omnipotence. And when these constellations of emotions intersect with the churning, manic depressive mood gyrations of the market itself, the result can be financially dangerous.

In other words, each of us—*including every Zen Millionaire*—has a darkside that can be "financially dangerous" in very subtle ways in today's hyper-frantic 24/7 financial markets.

In fact, your darkside lies in wait forever. So cunning is your darkside that it may convince you that you are engaging in positive, ethical behaviors intended to make you happy and financially successful. For example, look closely, you may see some of yourself in these six types of darkside personalities, which Schott believes undermine our path to financial success:

1. Certainty seekers. Can't deal with unpredictability. Hates risk, seeks safety. Becomes too cautious and conservative.

2. Hi-Anxiety Worriers. Perfectionists, must make the "right decision," and are indecisive, delay too long, or avoid decisions altogether.

3. Impulse Buyers. Needs a quick fix. Falls in and out of love fast. Bad at timing short-term market swings and long-term economic cycles.

4. Power Players. Fearless controllers. Market success makes them feel like a hero, while they deny, hide and laugh off their failures.

5. Gamblers. Loves thrill of playing the market. Addicted to the game. In a perverse way, they need to lose, to confirm a lack of self worth.

6. Survivor's Guilt. Feel undeserving. Prosperity contradicts lack of self-worth, so they are deeply conflicted by achieving wealth and success.

See yourself? The challenge of the darkside is much bigger than you can imagine. Think about it for a minute: If you have a secret that's hidden even from yourself, a secret that's sabotaging your life, a secret keeping you from being a whole person, a secret denying you a peaceful, happy, rich life—how can you possibly admit that *you* are this secret enemy hiding within your soul?

Wresting with the devil—or with God?

There is yet an even bigger challenge: If this secret saboteur does exist in you, it shares the same space within you, along side the "secret power within." And if that's true, you're in a no-win predicament! For how do you know which one is speaking, is guiding you—your Higher Self, or the darkside?

In this situation, at any moment in your struggle, how do you know if you are walking with God—or wrestling with the devil? Often you just do not know, there is no clear channel. Secrets are secrets. Enlightenment, like your million bucks, takes time ... even for The Buddha himself as Peck tells us:

> **Buddha found enlightenment only when he stopped seeking for it—when he let it come to him. On the other hand, who can doubt that enlightenment came to him precisely because he had devoted at least sixteen years of his life to seeking it, sixteen years in preparation.**

In other words, if you're on the path of a Zen Millionaire you must be patient, focused, disciplined. And yet, at the same time, you must accept the reality of living in an imperfect world. There's a great lesson on this in *The Spirituality of Imperfection* by Ernest Kurtz and Katherine Ketchham, a powerful lesson on dealing with a life of inconsistencies, contradictions, dilemmas, paradoxes and other unanswerable questions:

> **The core paradox that underlies spirituality is the haunting sense of incompleteness, of being somehow *unfinished,* that comes from the reality of living on this earth as part and yet also not-part of it. For to be human is to be incomplete, yet yearn for completion; it is to be uncertain, yet long for certainty; to be imperfect, yet long for perfection, to be broken, yet crave wholeness.**
>
> **All these yearnings remain necessarily unsatisfied, for perfection, completion, certainty, and wholeness are impossible precisely because we *are* imperfectly human—or better, because we are perfectly human, which is to say, humanly imperfect.**
>
> **This is the essential paradox of human life: We are always and inevitably incomplete, on the way, slipping and sliding, making mistakes. But the ancient voices insist that this is not failure; it is rather the necessary reflection of the paradox that we are.**

Unfortunately, the competitive Western culture you live in focuses too much on perfection, often obsessed with the notion of eliminating imperfections. In *Care of The Soul,* psychologist and former priest, Thomas Moore cautions us, offering a more balanced solution:

> **Modern psychologies and therapies often contain an unspoken but clear salvational tone. If you could only learn to be assertive, loving, angry, expressive, contemplative, or thin, they imply, your troubles would be over...**

> **It is commonplace for writers to point out that we live in a time of deep division, in which mind is separated from body and spirituality is at odds with materialism. But how do we get out of this split? We can't just 'think' ourselves through it, because thinking itself is part of the problem. What we need is a way out of our dualistic attitudes.**

Our culture's obsession with consumer spending, material success and quick fixes is relentlessly painted in television advertisements that separate us from our inner reality. In focusing on material things we not only widen the gap between our selves and the rest of the world as we consume a disproportionate share of the world's resources, we also become alienated from our true identity as spiritual beings. Moore says:

> **We need a third possibility, and that third is soul ... Care of the soul is quite different in scope from most modern notions of psychology and psychotherapy. It isn't about curing, fixing, changing, adjusting or making healthy, and it isn't about perfection. It doesn't look to the future for an ideal, trouble-free existence. Rather, it remains patiently in the present, close to life as it presents itself day by day, and yet at the same time mindful of religion and spirituality.**

> **Observance of the soul can be deceptively simple. You take back what has been disowned. You work with what is, rather than what you wish were there ... Therapy sometimes emphasizes change so strongly that people often neglect their own natures and are tantalized by**

images of some ideal normality and health that may always be out of reach.

You take back what you are disowning, denying, hiding. There is no split in Moore's view: Mind and body are not separate. Getting rich in fact is the same as getting rich in spirit. There is no split. You are one whole person. And there is nothing to fix. You stop trying to cure a problem that doesn't exist.

The Way of the Wizard—owning the shadow

There is a way out of the paradox. Echoing Moore and others, Deepak Chopra describes the path in *The Way of The Wizard:*

We all have a shadow self that is a part of our total reality. The shadow is not here to hurt you but to point out where you are incomplete. When the shadow is embraced, it can be healed. When it is healed it can turn into love. When you can live with your opposite qualities, you will be living your total self as a wizard.

Most of our darkside secrets are tied to childhood trauma that we may come to understand, although they may never disappear. You can learn to accept and deal with their effects on you in adulthood, but the memories linger, if in the shadows, haunting you, occasionally surfacing, surprising you like a ninja warrior, sabotaging your best efforts in the present, even after long periods hidden in the shadows.

Deal the cards, now—bet on your strengths

The Zen Millionaire accepts this shadowy aspect of their humanness. And one of the best ways of working through this challenge is to focus on the positive, while not denying the negative.

Marcus Buckingham, author of *First, Break All The Rules,* and *Now, Discover Your Strengths* put it this way in a *Fortune* magazine interview whimsically titled "Trying to overcome a weakness?

Please, stop!" The lesson applies equally to individuals as well as companies:

> **Most training is remedial, and when training is remedial, it's a waste of time. What companies need to be able to do is figure out where someone's natural talents lie, and then combine them with skills and knowledge … Imagine that you've got a deck of cards that's all shuffled. What are the top five cards that you're going to play? If you know those, you're in a much better position to be able to alter your career:** *Focus on your style and play to those strengths.*

In the final analysis, when you are all alone, the Zen Millionaire knows that the darkside is not "out there." It is within your soul—*it is you!* And as you look within, as you own it, you no longer see the darkside as a mysterious saboteur, but as a partner, your ally, your spirit and a great source of strength because "you come to bless the darkness as you bless the light."

Ninth Secret

YOU ARE THE ONLY GURU

IF YOU MEET THE BUDDHA ON THE ROAD

ON WALL STREET
ON CABLE TV
ONLINE
"KILL'EM!"

We're often told that "experience is the best teacher." In fact, the Buddha was quite clear about this principle: "Believe nothing, no matter where you read it or who has said it, not even if I have said it, unless it agrees with your own reason and your own common sense."

Many masters since then have underscored his message with yet another very familiar statement the ancient Zen masters—if you meet the Buddha on the road, kill him. The psychiatrist Sheldon Kopp even used this warning as the title of one of his books:

No meaning that comes from outside of ourselves is real. The Buddhahood of each of us has already been obtained. We need only recognize it. Thus the Zen Master warns his disciple: If you meet the Buddha on the road, kill him.

The importance of this principle should be obvious, especially to anyone on the path of the Zen Millionaire. Yet surprisingly, in America today, few grasp the message! In *The Way of Zen,* Alan Watts makes clear the challenge we all face:

> **Since one's own true nature is already Buddha nature, one does not have to do anything to make it so. On the contrary, to seek to become Buddha is to deny that one is already Buddha—and this is the sole basis upon which Buddhahood can be realized. In short, to become a Buddha it is only necessary to have the faith that one is a Buddha already.**

So if you meet him out there on Wall Street, anywhere, "kill 'em!" Not literally, of course. But you get it. There are no Buddhas "out there." Kill *the illusion* that there is someone who will take responsibility for your life, someone other than you, someone you can blame when things go wrong, as they will.

Wall Street gurus want you to be dependent

There are powerful forces throughout Wall Street, anywhere, and Corporate America that are tirelessly working to convince individual investors like you and me that they have better answers, quicker fixes, and solutions born of an expertise that is superior to yours. They want you to believe they have the ultimate truth, that they are the one True Buddha when it comes to your money, not you. Here's how to spot some of these Faux Buddhas:

- **Brokers (churning portfolios for big fees, commissions)**
- **Money managers (they charge big fees on your portfolio)**
- **Online traders (you lose as they make money on volume)**
- **Financial advisers (watch for undisclosed kickbacks)**
- **Mutual funds data trackers (information that's delayed, old, incomplete)**
- **Press and news media (sell magazines, newspapers, attract advertisers)**
- **Advertisers (your vulnerability keeps them in business)**

In a metaphoric sense, the financial world is a nationwide, amoral conspiracy operating in direct opposition to the principles and strategies of the emerging new Zen Millionaire.

As a result, many of the new players in today's fast-paced money game hesitate, confused, frustrated, doubting the secret power within them. Often, they just give up and surrender to the "Buddha out there." Jerry Tweddell and Jack Pierce describe this deception in *Winning with Index Mutual Funds:*

> **Investors are reluctant to attempt do-it-yourself investing, because they view it as too 'serious' an undertaking. Brokers spend millions of advertising dollars encouraging that very notion: Investors are helplessly adrift on stormy seas, desperately in need of an expert and experienced hand at the helm—which only Wall Street can provide.**

Wall Street's leading firm, Morgan Stanley, regularly sells this illusion of superiority. Years ago one of their ads even bragged that: "If God wanted an investment banker, he'd hire Morgan Stanley." And not long ago they ran an ad carrying this arrogant message, "Wall Street can do it better than Main Street." In short, they want to brainwash you into believing that Wall Street's experts are the real Buddha, and you should surrender to them, become dependent on them. Notice their holier-than-thou tone, which is in direct opposition to all the principles in this book:

> **Life's not fair. Being smart doesn't necessarily make you a financial success. Believing in yourself only goes so far. You can work and save your money and still be surpassed by people who simply put their money in a better place ... That place? Morgan Stanley.**

The culture of America's financial community is stuck in an arrogant medieval mindset, a time when only the high priests had the ear of God, and mere mortals surrendered their power to these priests, gurus, wizards, experts and miscellaneous external authorities. By divine right, they were entrusted with the power of doing your thinking for you. God gave them the power. You just don't have what it takes.

That same culture continues today, constantly reinforced in the news and advertising media: They want you to believe you are a child, and you should accept that they are a benevolent parent who knows what's best for you.

David wins because Goliath is an illusion

While self-interest drives Wall Street, some insiders not only challenge the greed and absence of morality driving it, but they puncture massive holes in the illusion that Wall Street can invest your money better than you. Burton Malkiel, a former governor of the American Stock Exchange and member of the Council of Economic Advisors was rather blunt about this fact in his classic, *A Random Walk Down Wall Street:*

> **Many people say that the individual investor has scarcely a chance today against Wall Street's pros … that there is no longer any room for the individual investor in today's institutionalized markets. Nothing could be further from the truth. You can do it as well as the experts—perhaps even better.**

The Zen Millionaire knows this instinctively, but the distractions are many and relentlessly coming at you as Wall Street spends more than $15 billion annually to get you to doubt yourself.

Take a peek behind the curtain, see the real wizard

Don't be distracted: Like Dorothy in The Wizard of Oz, take a peek behind the curtain, you will find a pretender every time. Know who you are: You are a millionaire-in-training with all the skills, knowledge and the right state of mind to invest successfully—as good as or better than Wall Street's wizards hidden behind the curtains of their advertisements.

Remember, the Buddha is within you! Not out there on Wall Street, or on CNBC, or in Forbes, Fortune or The Journal. Trust yourself. You really do know what's best for you. Act with confidence, learn from mistakes, and over time you will improve your skills through experience. But you must take charge. As martial arts champion and film hero Chuck Norris put it in *The Secret Power Within:*

> **I have always been struck by the strong resemblance between those first steps of Zen and life itself. If you really want something, you must go after it yourself, and with all your dedication.**

The Zen Millionaire knows this: No one can do it for you. Ever. If you want anything, you must go after it, trusting the secret power within. If you turn your power over to external authorities you are splitting yourself, weakening yourself, creating more problems, more frustrations, more suffering.

Know that you alone are responsible. And they are not to blame, even if you give them your power. You're stuck with the results, no matter what. The gurus you give your power to are just projections of your self-doubts. If you ever see a Buddha on the road, know that it is only a reflection in a cracked mirror, a false Buddha—you are giving away your soul.

You are the only guru—do it yourself!

If you meet the Buddha in the road, on Wall Street or CNBC, "kill 'em!" The Christian mystics Meister Eckhart and St. Francis put it in gentler terms: "What you are looking for, you are looking with."

Know that the Creator is within you. The Kingdom is within you. The secret power is within you. The *only* Buddha you will ever "see" is the Buddha within you, projected onto a world full of gurus competing for power. The Zen Millionaire sees through this world, knows that the only expert, the only guru, the only Buddha, is within you—so take charge, do it yourself.

PART FOUR

BOOTCAMP
FOR
TRANSFORMATION
GET TOUGH! GET ZEN! GET RICH!

In bootcamp, kids grow up fast, become disciplined fighters. I remember my days in the United States Marine Corps bootcamp. A set of tough principles gets imbedded in your brain fast—for living, for staying alive, for survival in the real world—and for growing spiritually.

But when it comes to money, most Americans don't learn the right lessons early enough, many never do. The millionaires bootcamp is designed to prepare you for the daily cultural war you must live in—a highly competitive world hell-bent on brainwashing us, programming us with a killer instinct, an obsession with material success, an anxiety craving instant gratification.

In bootcamp you move from tough principles to the gentle practice of those principles, learning how to win big in the competitive jungle of Wall Street and Corporate America, while never surrendering your integrity, values and principles.

There are no tough sergeants here. I'm no guru, not a master, teacher, or a Marine sergeant any more. Yes, I did my doctoral dissertation on transformational psychology and studied with the Zen Millionaire. But I really haven't mastered the training, just another beginner trudging the path, what you might call a "Flawed Buddha." You volunteered to come here, to learn these principles, so the work is totally up to you; perhaps my experience will help you.

THE
JOURNEY
OF SELF-DISCOVERY
NEVER ENDS

You are on a journey that never ends—into the sunlight, lost in a dark forest, always chasing a moving target. New careers, public recognition, a loving marriage, wonderful children, good health, supportive friends, a million dollars. Then often, when you least expect it, more surprises, new challenges, business crises, sudden endings, dislocations, the loss of a loved one—and every step along the way, struggling to renew your conscious contact with the mysterious forces of the universe that give meaning to your life.

Eventually you come to expect the unexpected, understand how to deal with the good and bad in life, and grow through all of life's cycles, the ups, and the downs. In time you begin to welcome each new adventure with the enthusiasm of a modern day Ralph Waldo Emerson:

Do not go where the path may lead.
Go instead where there is no path,
and leave a trail.

One of the great paradoxes of your journey is that while you must travel alone, at the same time you know you are being guided. Napoleon Hill, the author of *Think And Grow Rich* wrote about his sense of awe in one of his later books when he discovered that every one of the five hundred successful men in his research knew they were guided by "unknown sources," and that knowledge gave them confidence to go their own way.

Surprises are part of every journey: You are amazed as the journey unfolds, as unexpected opportunities to grow and change become a natural part of everyday life. In his book, *The Way of Transition,* the psychologist William Bridges reminds us of life's sudden twists and turns pushing us into new worlds of opportunity and challenge:

> **It's an age-old story: You think you are heading for India, and you end up in the West Indies. You run after the ball, and you fall down the rabbit hole. You're a prehistoric fish in a dried-up sea that's just trying to flop across the mud to a new puddle, and the next thing you know you're breathing air!**

> **You think you're doing one thing, and all of the time you're busy doing another. Many of the biggest transformations come when you think that you're just trying to reestablish the status quo.**

No one understood better than Joseph Campbell the journey each of us must make in our lifetime. His work has helped millions. It was my good fortune to be at one of Campbell's "Mythical Meditation" seminars in a New York Soho loft. I fell down the rabbit hole and my entire life suddenly went in a whole new direction, from Wall Street to Hollywood.

The journey of the hero—alone with everyone

Many books have been written by and about Campbell. One of the best is *The Power of Myth,* transcripts of interviews by Bill Moyers at the Skywalker Ranch, the home of George Lucas, the director of StarWars. In the chapter on "The Hero's Journey" Campbell talks about the bizarre journey each of us is making:

> **Furthermore, we have not even to risk the adventure alone, for the heroes of all time have gone before us. The labyrinth is thoroughly known. We have only to**

follow the thread of the hero path, and where we had thought to find an abomination, we shall find a god. And where we had thought to slay another, we shall slay ourselves. Where we had thought to travel outward, we will come to the center of our existence. And where we had thought to be alone, we will be with all the world.

This is important, so listen closely: Campbell is saying that the still small voice within you is telling you that your journey is "thoroughly known" by you, in advance. That is why the Zen Millionaire, once on this path, already knows everything said here, before reading it.

This book is merely a reminder for the rough days when you feel alone. You are never alone, you are a whole person, at one with the world, linked to the same "unseen guides" Napoleon Hill's 500 business and financial leaders each discovered by themselves. Guided, yes, but still left with an awesome awareness that you must make this journey alone. In *The Road Less Traveled* the psychiatrist Scott Peck describes this journey for all travelers:

Our journey of spiritual growth is guided by the invisible hand and unimaginable wisdom of God with infinitely greater accuracy than that of our unaided conscious will is capable ... While the words of the prophets and the assistance of grace are available, the journey must still be traveled alone. No teacher can carry you ... No teaching can be taught that will relieve spiritual travelers from the necessity of picking their own ways, working out with effort and anxiety their own paths through the unique circumstances of their own lives toward the identification of their individual selves with God.

You know in your heart that your journey through life is a spiritual journey, that you are a spiritual being having a human experience, that you are on a life-long quest, not to discover "the meaning of life," but rather to add meaning to your life. Campbell's *Journey of the Hero* is at the center of all life:

A hero is someone who has given his or her life to something bigger oneself ... The hero's journey always

begins with the call. One way or another, a guide must come to say, 'Look, you're in Sleepy Land. Wake. Come on a trip. There is a whole aspect of your consciousness, your being, that's not enough.' And so it starts.

The call is to leave a certain social situation, move into your loneliness and find the jewel, the center that's impossible to find when you're socially engaged. You are thrown off-center, and when you feel off-center, it's time to go.

Campbell often uses the mythic search for the Holy Grail from the adventures of King Arthur's Knights of the Roundtable as the archetypal example of the hero's journey, of your journey and mine:

What the Holy Grail symbolizes is the highest spiritual fulfillment of a human life. Each life has some kind of high fulfillment, and has its own gift ....

In the story of Sir Galahad, the knights agree to go on a quest, but thinking it would be a disgrace to go forth in a group, each entered the forest, at one point or another, where they saw it to be thickest, all in those places where they found no way or path.

Where there is a path, it's someone else's path. Each knight enters the forest at the most mysterious point and follows his own intuition. What each brings forth is what never before was on land or sea: the fulfillment of his unique potentialities, which are different from anybody else's.

So your journey begins with an inner calling, often brought on by some external event that throws you off-course. Then, suddenly you know "it is time for you to go," although at the outset you probably don't know where.

Your adventure into the "zone unknown"

Thus, our journey, yours, mine, everyone's journey, parallels the mythic adventures of the knights in search of the Holy Grail—a long journey into the dark forest where there is no path, only the one you make, where there is no meaning, only the meaning that you ultimately bring to life:

> **Whenever a knight of the Grail tried to follow a path made by someone else, he went altogether astray. Where there is a way or path, it is someone else's footsteps. Each of us has to find his own way ... The call to adventure signifies that destiny has summoned the hero and transferred his spiritual center of gravity from within the pale of society to the *zone unknown.***

For the Zen Millionaire, the "zone unknown" is the battleground of money, personal finance, economics and wealth-building ... it is Wall Street, the Dow Industrials and SEC ... mortgages, insurance and credit cards ... for the Zen Millionaire the "zone unknown" is an incredible opportunity to discover the meaning of life, of your life ... while also accumulating a million dollar net worth. And on that path, you discover that the secret power within you and the mysterious creative forces of the universe have much in common.

Eleventh Secret

MAKE A DIFFERENCE GET RICH ENRICH THE WORLD

The ancient masters tell us that when you're enlightened, everyone's enlightened. When you are a Zen Millionaire, everyone is one. You see things differently, you make things happen.

In this sense, a Zen Millionaire is a contradiction, a paradox, a koan, an impossible question, a perfect example of the Zen that cannot be described in words, yet is so obvious. What a wonderful opportunity for a full life, for spiritual growth and psychological wholeness. A million dollar net worth—*and a life in service to the world.* Proof you can have it all this lifetime.

Your life's work will be your path to enriching the world. In *The Three Pillars of Zen,* Philip Kapleau, an American Zen master, wrote of the absolute connection between Zen, enlightenment and the world around you, where your life's work is...

ennobling because it is seen as an expression of the immaculate Buddha-nature. This is true enlightenment, and enlightenment in Zen is never for oneself alone but for the sake of all.

Please understand the profound import of his message: Your career, your work, your money, even enlightenment is not for you alone. They are gifts to be shared and passed on. You have a responsibility to serve the world, beyond merely accumulating a million dollar net worth. Eventually, this responsibility to the world transcends all others. It is everywhere recognized as one of the highest of human tasks:

The Buddha. **Strive constantly to serve the welfare of the world; by devotion to selfless work one attains the supreme goal of life.**

Winston Churchill. **We make a living by what we get, we make a life by what we give.**

Oprah Winfrey. **We each should allow our excellence to come forth and serve the world.**

Deepak Chopra. **Everyone has a purpose in life, a unique gift of special talent to give others ... Discover your divinity, find your unique talent, serve humanity with it, and you can generate all the wealth you want.**

You were born into a culture where money can easily become a destructive rather than enlightening influence. Indeed, the truth is that wealth is more often than not an enemy of the spiritual life, rather than an ally, which is why monks in the East and West traditionally take vows of poverty, refusing to accumulate wealth, begging for food to assure that nothing blocks their spiritual journey.

But just as you can be too materialistic, you can also become too spiritual, and acquire the "stink of Zen," a term ancient masters used to describe anyone whose ego gets caught up in the pomp and rituals, dogma, pretensions, slogans, and other outward trappings of whatever "ism" they belonged to at the time.

The world needs you rich in spirit *and in fact!*

Most of us don't have the luxury of monastic isolation. Out in the real world there are few easy escapes, we *must* earn money and accumulate wealth, while trying hard not to lose our spiritual nature.

We know firsthand that money can be either corrupting or ennobling. And looking at the world as an optimist, it appears that for most people, money is ennobling. But neither path is locked in your genes. You must make this tough choice all by yourself, says the philosopher, Jacob Needleman, author of *Money and the Meaning of Life:*

> **Ralph Waldo Emerson wrote, 'Man is born to be rich.' He didn't mean being a fat cat, but he meant human beings are born to experience as much as the earth has to offer, and money helps. In that way, money is a tremendously good thing. It's just when it becomes our master that it's deadly.**

The economist Paul Zane Pilzer also offers a positive and balanced perspective of this human need to accept—*and live with*—the dangers of juggling money with the higher rewards of the spirit, rather than run away from the challenge and hide from reality.

In *God Wants You To Be Rich,* Pilzer makes it clear that from his perspective as an economist, wealth is not only part of each individual's spiritual path, but wealth has a higher purpose—your wealth, my wealth, our collective wealth, benefits the entire world. Listen to this radical position:

> **God does want each of us to be rich in every possible way—health, love, and peace of mind, as well as material possessions. God wants this, however, not just for our own sake, but for the sake of all humankind. An increase in the wealth for an individual almost always represents an even larger increase in wealth for society at large.**

Of course this vision is at odds with the conventional wisdom of our culture. From this vantage point, not only is money essential to your spiritual journey, and not only will an increase in individual wealth benefit the world, but the Zen Millionaire has a *moral obligation to* increase their personal wealth in order to serve the world. That's right, the goal of getting rich is actually a spiritual, social, moral and ethical obligation, part of the contract that you agreed to before coming into this life.

Collective consciousness and the revolution

As radical as this obligation may seem, this principle is becoming widely understood and accepted. In *Real Magic,* Wayne Dyer describes this sweeping trend as signaling a global shift from the "collective unconscious" in Jung's psychology to a new "collective consciousness" and a worldwide transformation:

> **There is a new collective consciousness in the minds of people, and a new spiritual awareness is spreading throughout humanity. Nothing can stop it, for nothing is more powerful than an *idea* whose time has come. An idea is a thought—individual or collective—that, once spread to enough souls, manifests in physical changes …**

> **Now we see a new reality, a reality that comes from a new way of thinking, and this is the context of our spiritual revolution. This new way of thinking is consequently a new way of being for humanity.**

The Dalai Lama also speaks of an emerging worldwide spiritual revolution in *Ethics for the New Millennium:*

> **A revolution is called for, certainly. But not a political, an economic, even a technical revolution. We have enough experience of the past century to know that a purely external approach will not suffice. What I propose is a spiritual revolution.**

> **In calling for a spiritual revolution, am I advocating a religious solution to our problems after all? No … I have come to the conclusion that whether or not a person is a religious believer does not matter much. Far more important is that they be a good person. … We humans can live quite well without recourse to religious faith.**

> **My call for a spiritual revolution is thus not a call for a religious revolution. Nor is it a reference to a way of life that is somehow otherworldly, still less to something magical or mysterious. Rather it is a call for a radical**

reorientation away from our habitual preoccupation with self. It is a call to turn toward the wider community of beings with whom we are connected, and for conduct which recognizes other's interests alongside our own.

When you are a Zen Millionaire, everyone is one. You have a responsibility, an obligation, a duty to accumulate wealth, for yourself, and for the good of the whole world.

Balancing the material with a spiritual revolution

You know you are at one with these revolutionaries being called into action by the Dalai Lama. You also know the Zen Millionaire's path is a huge challenge because doing things for the good of everyone often comes after taking care of life's more immediate demands, in particular, family obligations. Here's how Lee & MacKenzie described this balancing act in their book about millionaires, *Getting Rich in America:*

> **All you have to do is recognize the opportunities that abound around you and work to seize a share of those opportunities; develop a long-term perspective; work and study hard; be reasonably frugal and judicious in your purchases; get married and stay married; take care of yourself; accept prudent risks and invest wisely— but above all, be patient. But that's a tall order ... given that most Americans have so little net worth when they end their careers.**

Fear not, you are not being called to "save the world" as a missionary. Your responsibility is first to yourself and your inner power. No Zen, no millionaire-in-training, no secret power within, no you.

Selfishness, selflessness and the common good

Of course all this will seem incredibly selfish to monks living in monasteries under strict rules that forbid personal wealth accumulation. That's alright, that's their path, not yours. The path of the Zen Millionaire is more of a contrarian, a "universal individualist who is never a member of any Zen organization," as Alan Watts describes it.

You must honor *your* calling. Your calling may be small or large—raising a family or transforming a nation—but it must be *your* calling. And your calling must be honored first—then your responsibility to the world will be obvious and will flow naturally in your life and work. Ralph Waldo Emerson put it quite poetically:

Success. To laugh often and much; to win the respect of intelligent people and the affection of children; to earn the appreciation of honest critics and endure the betrayal of false friends; to appreciate beauty, to find the best in others; to leave the world a bit better, whether by a healthy child, a garden patch or a redeemed social condition; to know even one has breathed easier because you have lived. This is to have succeeded.

You travel down the road less traveled, on a journey where few have gone. And in the process, you get rich not just for your own sake, but you do it for the sake of all humankind.

Leap ... and the net will appear

Ask and you shall receive. Not *maybe* receive, you *shall* receive! Surrender to that certainty. Trust. Here's how Julie Cameron put it in *The Artist's Way:* "Leap and the net will appear." If you believe, if you trust, if you want it, know that you have it all, now, for you are already a Zen Millionaire. Gary Zukav offers one of the most enlightened descriptions of this total surrender in *The Seat of The Soul:*

Let go of what you think is just reward. Let go. Trust. Create. Be who you are. The rest is up to your nonphysical Teachers and the Universe.

Take your hands off the wheel. Be able to say to the Universe, 'Thy will be done,' and allow your life to go into the hands of the Universe completely. The final piece of reaching for authentic power is releasing your own to a higher form of wisdom...

Release your specifications and say to the Universe: 'Find me where you know I need to be.' Let them go and trust that the Universe will provide, and so it shall. Let go of all. Let your higher self complete its task.

Surrender to this universal power, for when you are a Zen Millionaire, everyone is a Zen Millionaire because you have a new world vision, you are in service to the world around you, making a difference, and enriching the whole world with your unique gifts.

THE
SECRET POWER
IS WITHIN YOU

SO IS THE KINGDOM
THE BUDDHA, THE CREATOR
THE MASTERMIND
THE UNIVERSE
TRUST IT

This is as spiritual as it gets—*when you are rich in spirit, you are rich in fact.* Neither avoiding money in a monastery, nor dependent on outside authorities telling you what to do about money, nor obsessively playing the money game out there, on Wall Street and in Corporate America. The Zen Millionaire welcomes the opportunities and challenges that arrive daily when you're getting rich in fact *and in spirit.*

The only issue is whether you will deal with each new test with the same spirit of integrity and equanimity as the last, growing through each. The Zen Millionaire accepts this seemingly endless daily struggle, facing life with some of the same sense of anticipation, wonder and excitement that lit the way for Joseph Campbell:

Follow your bliss and doors will open where there were no doors before … When you look back on your life, it looks as though it were a plot, but when you are into it, it's a mess: just one surprise after another. Then later, you see it was perfect. So, I have a theory that if you are on your path, things are going to come to you. Since it's your own path, and no one has ever been on it before,

there's no precedent, so everything that happens is a surprise and is timely.

The Zen Millionaire knows from deep within that what you are looking *for,* you're looking *with,* what you are searching for, you already have within you.

Remember, it's your life, you are responsible, you are in charge—not some financial guru, expert or anchor "out there" telling you what they want you to do. The "it" you seek is with you now, all day, every day. Even when you are not thinking about it, it is thinking about you, protecting you, so let go and know you are protected and guided—even when things look messy.

Money has no power over you—the power is within you. Trust it. We are not talking about financial and economic power, but the spiritual power that binds you with the Universal Creator, with the Kingdom that is within you. With the Creator in you. The Buddha within you. With everything.

The secret is—there is no secret

You are one with the great mysteries of the Tao, the Kingdom within, Universal Energy, Ki, your Higher Power, the Force, your Creator, Yahweh, Gaia, Nature, God. This is the vastness of the spirit of Zen. It is very much alive and well within you. *You are it—and it is you.* In *This Thing Called You,* Dr. Ernest Holmes, founder of Science of Mind, reminds us that:

> **Every man is a doorway, as Emerson said, through which the Infinite passes into the finite, through which God becomes man, through which the Universal becomes individual.**

Similarly, in his book, *If You Meet The Buddha on The Road, Kill Him,* the psychiatrist Sheldon B. Kopp tells us just how obvious, visible and unmysterious Zen is in our everyday lives:

> **While seeking to be taught the Truth, the disciple learns only that there is nothing that anyone else can teach**

> him. He learns, once he is willing to give up being taught, that he already knows how to live, that it is implied in his own tale. The secret is that there is no secret.
>
> Everything is just what it seems to be. This is it. There are no hidden meanings ... The Zen way to see the truth is through your everyday eyes. It is only the heartless questioning of life-as-it-is that ties a man in knots. A man does not need an answer in order to find peace. He needs only to surrender to his existence, to cease the needless, empty questioning. The secret of enlightenment is when you are hungry, eat, and when you are tired, sleep.

There is no secret to life, nor to playing the money game: You're it. You and it are one. You have the power to get rich in fact as well as in spirit, because the power is within you, and always has been.

This is as spiritual as it gets—the secret power is within

This truly is as spiritual as it gets. You are playing the game of life guided by a secret identical to the one that sustained Carl Jung from early childhood—a secret so powerful and so personal he waited to reveal it in his autobiography, *Memories, Dreams, Reflections,* published after his death:

> I find that all my thoughts circle around God like the planets around the sun, and are irresistibly attracted to Him ... I knew what God's grace was. One must be utterly abandoned to God; nothing matters but fulfilling His will. I knew, knew from experience, that this grace was accorded only to one who fulfilled the will of God without reservation ... To me it seemed that one's duty was to explore daily the will of God ... I must take responsibility, it was up to me how my fate turned out ... I had to find the answer out of my deepest self, that I was alone before God ... Nobody could rob me of the conviction that it was enjoined upon me to do what God wanted and not what I wanted. That gave me the strength to go my own way. Often I had the feeling that

in all decisive matters I was no longer among men, but was alone with God. And when I was 'there,' where I was no longer alone, I was outside time; I belonged to the centuries; and He who then gave the answer was He who had always been, who had been before my birth. He who always is was there.

In the final analysis, this is as spiritual as it gets for a Zen Millionaire trudging on the long journey to a million dollar net worth. When you have the Zen, you know the secret. You are a millionaire-in-training until you are a millionaire in fact. *But you are a Zen Millionaire now, today, at this moment, every step of way.* And no one needs to know that but you. You just do what you know you must do, trusting the universe, knowing with certainty that you are guided, just as Jung knew his destiny.

The American dollar bill is a daily reminder of the spirituality of money. Every time we dig into our wallets we see: "In God We Trust!" Be grateful you are a Zen Millionaire, working on the million, living in the spirit of Zen, in tune with the secret power within you.

This is as spiritual as it gets—you are playing the money game every day, with integrity, doing the right thing, and you know deep within your soul that *you are already rich—rich in spirit, rich in fact!*

POSTSCRIPTS

- **10 Quick Steps Inside a Millionaire's Mindset**

- **The Incredibles Fab-u-lous Retirement Formula**

- **The 12-Step Program for Financial Peace**

10 QUICK STEPS INSIDE A MILLIONAIRE'S MIND

The Wall Street Journal

A DataMonitor study says the number of American millionaires rose from 7.3 million in 2002 to 8.5 million in 2004. At the current 7.1% annual growth rate, we're creating a million new millionaires every year, a total of 12 million millionaires by 2008. That's ten million new opportunities every decade.

You can become a millionaire! Here's the secret: It's all in your head, your attitude, your state of mind. If you want to retire a millionaire, you can. You control your mind. A few decades in business convinced me of this one simple truth: Becoming a millionaire is all in your head. It has little to do with wealth-building techniques, tools and rules.

In fact, you could even forget all the usual stuff: asset allocation, stock picking, savings plans, budgeting, and so on. I know that's what advisers, pundits, brokers and other experts tell you to focus on. But if you're not in the right state of mind, none of that matters.

Seriously, I've read all the books: *The Millionaire Mind, Instant Millionaire, Automatic Millionaire, Millionaire Next Door, One Minute Millionaire,* and many more. Even wrote one, *The Millionaire Code,* and worked on Wall Street with Morgan Stanley for many years.

But I keep coming back to this one simple fact: It really is all in your head! Period. No excuses. Here are the 10 best tips I picked up over the decades, tips that'll help you become one of America's next millionaires.

1. Getting rich isn't about money

Peter Lynch says if you spend 15 minutes a year studying the economy, that's 10 minutes too much. And when money guru Ric Edelman researched 5,000 millionaires for *Ordinary People, Extraordinary Wealth*, he discovered that millionaires spend an average of just six minutes a day on personal finance. They have better things to do. Get a life!

2. Accentuate the positive

Most of us have read books like *Success Through a Positive Mental Attitude*. That message was summarized for me by a Special Forces instructor, a veteran of 26 years: "If you have a guy with all the survival training in the world who has a negative attitude and a guy who doesn't have a clue but has a positive attitude, I guarantee you that the guy with a positive attitude is coming out of the woods alive. Simple as that."

3. Think different

Go inside *The Millionaire Mind* with author George Stanley: "They think differently from the crowd ... It pays to be different." Yes, it builds wealth. That's "the central theme" of his work: Don't fit in, go your way.

4. Quit doing what you hate

Many people live in quiet desperation, waiting for retirement, doing something they hate. Marcus Buckingham put it very simply in his new book, *The One Thing You Need to Know*: Figure out what you don't like doing, then stop doing it.

5. Do what you love

You've heard all the pep talks: Follow your bliss; do what you love, money will follow. Never forget Stanley's bottom line: "If you are creative enough to select the ideal vocation, you can win, win big-time. The really brilliant millionaires are those who selected a vocation that they love."

6. Find 'the real you!'

Working in career that doesn't fit right is exhausting and stressful. You're less efficient, less productive, and underperform. Get in sync with the real you. Get help from a career counselor. Read books on personality types. In *The Millionaire Code* I identify 16 basic types to help people focus on their dreams. Buckingham's *Now Discover Your Strengths* is another example. Find the real you, go for it and never turn back!

7. Invest in "You, Inc."

Tired of working for Corporate America? Become an entrepreneur. Create your own business. Read Kiyosaki's *Rich Dad* series. Browse through *EBay for Dummies*. Open a BurgerKing franchise. Most millionaires work for themselves, pay less taxes, live below their means, and build equity in themselves.

8. Live with passion

Believe in something. Listen to the still small voice. What is it: Love, family, jazz, art, golf, writing, fishing, inventing? Whatever it is, it's you. And it's priceless. My mentor Joseph Campbell said: "If you follow your bliss, you will always have your bliss, money or not. If you follow money, you may lose it, and you will have nothing."

9. Live in the moment

A good friend is in his sixties. When I mention retirement planning, he laughs. He talks about his next vacation. His new jet-skis. He's survived divorce, bankruptcy, foreclosure, health problems. He has a successful business, nice house, lots of debt. He's at risk. I couldn't do it, but he's happy. We all have friends like him. You can only push so far. Then you let go and love them. We all live in the moment, that's his, live yours.

10. Make a difference!

Most of us focus on our little world and our future. Millionaires dream of making the world a better place, with visions of a better tomorrow for everyone. They love helping people. I'll bet you have such a dream. Discover the real meaning of life by going beyond yourself, and make a difference!

Remember, being a millionaire is all in your head. If you got the right attitude, if you feel it, if you believe you're a millionaire, you're already there. The money will follow. Trust it.

THE INCREDIBLES
ONE FAMILY'S FAB-U-LOUS
RETIREMENT FORMULA

The Wall Street Journal

You won't hear this on Wall Street. But here's a super-secret "Incredible Millionaires Retirement Formula." I didn't learn this during my years with Morgan Stanley or in law school. My grandparents taught me, by example. The kind of wisdom you don't appreciate until you grow up.

They raised me in a small town. Both retired. We lived off Grampa's garden in summer, Gramma's canning in winter. Their world was right out of the movie, "It's a Wonderful Life." We always had more than enough. Being rich never crossed my mind. I just ushered at the movies, clerked at the newsstand, played football, went to church, then off to the Marines, Hollywood and Wall Street.

Movies get us thinking. They help us find answers to today's challenges in yesterday's lessons, so we can make sense out of tomorrow. "The Incredibles" got me thinking about what being "rich" really meant to my grandparents. My brain made some interesting connections, and suddenly, out pops the "Incredible Millionaires Retirement Formula!"

But like I said, you won't hear this from Wall Street's brokers or financial advisers. Why? Because they're not superheroes, they're super-myopic. They make their living managing assets, by siphoning fees off the top. You get the leftovers. Their formula is very narrow: They say you need a million bucks in the bank to retire like a millionaire. A million invested at five percent generates $50,000 annually.

No, you don't need a million to retire like a millionaire

Wrong! Shift your focus: You need monthly cash flows, not a million bucks in assets. Moreover, our formula proves retirement is more a matter of attitude than assets. My grandparents left me with the belief that you can live rich and retire like millionaire, without lots of assets. It's more in your head, your heart, your soul. And whatever that feeling is, I got a big-time reminder from "The Incredibles" movie!

The Incredibles are a "typical" America family of four: Mr. Incredible is a retired superhero working for Corporate America in a typical boring job, in insurance. His wife, Elasti-Girl, another retired superhero, is a typical loving (not desperate!) housewife. They have two "typical" teenagers. Sweet, shy Violet feels invisible and she often is. And hyper-energetic Dash can run the 100-yards in the blink of an eye.

This family's loaded with super-powers. But they hide it. They're trying hard to be a typical American family, what society expects. Not super, not even above average. Just normal folks fitting in a society that encourages the mediocre rather than the exceptional. Then the challenge. Destiny calls. They're forced to reclaim their powers, become superheroes again and save the world! That inspired me.

Yes, anyone can have incredible superpowers

So I'm doctoring the script for you. Listen closely: I'll show you how you can capture the spirit of these four superheroes, get rich and retire like a millionaire. And do it without all the assets the Wall Street brainwashing machine wants you to think you need.

Forget Wall Street's asset-based formula. The "Incredible Millionaires Retirement Formula" focuses on cash flow. For example, let's say you need $4,000 a month. The American Association of Retired Persons (AARP) says most retirees live on less and yet are happy with their lives. So here's the new script. Here's how you can retire a millionaire in spirit and in fact.

Mr. Incredible's savings power

If you max out your IRA and your 401k every month starting at age thirty, with as little as $150 a month, compounding does the rest. Guaranteed millionaire. Okay, so yours is low? Stop beating yourself. Start where you are now. Save what you can. No big deal.

Violet's "invisible assets" power

Fixed pensions and Social Security benefits are better than hard assets in a volatile market. Step into Violet's secret world. See your "invisible assets." Suppose you and your spouse are getting a total of $2,500 monthly from Social Security. If you also get another $1,500 from pensions, you have the $4,000 you want. And you got it with nothing in savings! Get it?

Dash's high-energy work power

Have fun working part-time. Do what you always wanted, something you love. Seventy percent of retirees work. Most do it to keep busy, not because they have to. Everything from eBay auctions to Wal-Mart greeters, artists to entrepreneurs. In today's wonderful world of opportunities Dash's a cheerleader convinced you can make fast money every month.

Elasti-Mom's home ownership power

Home is where most families build their wealth quietly. Lotsa opportunities to streeeetch your dollars (and your thinking) says Elasti-Mom. Just don't waste this valuable asset on home equity loans. Keep your equity building. Later, you can pay down the mortgage, live debt-free. Or cash out and move to a smaller home, in a lower-cost area.

Now here's the big secret in the "Incredible Millionaires Retirement Formula." Add up everything from savings, pensions, Social Security, lower home costs, and a new career, and I'll bet you'll have the $50,000 you need annually in retirement. Notice: That's the same as having a million invested at five percent. That's the secret! You can retire a millionaire without a million bucks in the bank.

Amazing isn't it, what we learn from movies, super-heroes and grandparents about how simple money and investing really can be.

THE 12-STEP PROGRAM
FOR
FINANCIAL PEACE
HOW TO WIN IN BULL & BEAR MARKETS

The Wall Street Journal

When the stock market bears start growling, don't panic. You can keep your spirits up when the market indexes are down. I've learned over the past three decades that the euphoria of rising markets can be just as deadly to some investors as a night at the corner saloon can be to an alcoholic. You can't beat the feelings of watching your portfolio rise 20% or 30% in a year. It's great. You're the smartest guy in the room. You're witty, you're sexy, you're getting richer every day. You're at the top of your game.

Then, wham! The market takes a dive, and in a few short days or a week, the Dow Jones Industrial Average drops 400 to 500 points. It happens. And suddenly, you're frozen and can do nothing. Maybe worse, you try to buy your way out of the sell-off. But nothing you do makes a difference. Like hangovers, bear markets can come overnight and hang around for a long, long time. And they feel just as bad.

Who wants to live, or invest, that way? I sure didn't. I needed to break my up-down investing cycle, so I developed my own 12-step program that works for bull-market addicts just the way that other addicts have been aided by similar recovery plans.

Practice these principles and you too, could enjoying a sense of peace you'll never find by obsessing over the market's daily roller-coaster ride. (You'll be richer for it, too.)

Step 1: Admitted you are powerless over the market, that your portfolio is unmanageable.

Market cycles are totally unpredictable, and no one knows where the market is headed over the next few months or years. In *Stocks for the Long Run*, Wharton economist Jeremy Siegel researched the 120 largest up and down moves of the stock market from 1801 to 2001 and discovered that 75% of the tame there was no rational explanation for the moves.

Step 2: Think in decades, not quarters.

Yes, in the long run, markets go up. But short-term they're fickle, volatile and irrational. And they go down. Forget market timing, you'll lose. Dalbar, a Boston research firm, has followed mutual-fund investors for a couple decades and found that market timers *lost* an average of 3.29% annually while dollar-cost averagers made 6.8% a year. Lesson: Always bet on the long term.

Step 3: Turn to a "higher power," the market itself.

The best way to make sure your investments go up over the long term is a well-diversified asset-allocation strategy that mimics the market itself: Buy index funds that automatically adjust their holdings for you.

Step 4: Save 10%, or forget about retiring.

Think about market dips as huge wake-up calls. So let me repeat the warning: If you aren't putting away 10 cents out of every dollar you make, you're spending too much and you are not saving enough for retirement.

Step 5: Focus on your portfolio.

Whether you're a retiree, boomer or college kid, most of your portfolio's long-term performance depends on your asset allocations, not the specific funds you pick. For instance, William Bernstein's No-Brainer Portfolio returned about 14% in 2004 beating long-term averages of 12% annually. And it's simple: an equal mix of four Vanguard index funds: S&P 500 (VFINX); Small-Cap (NAESX);

European Stock (VEURX) and the Total Bond Market (VBMFX). Bernstein is a neurologist, money manager and author of *The Intelligent Asset Allocator.*

Step 6. Low turnovers lower your taxes and raise profits.
Actively-managed domestic stock funds turnover their entire portfolios more than 100% every year. The manager's transaction costs reduce your returns and increase your taxes. Buy funds with turnover ratios under 30%.

Step 7: Buy only no-load funds.
Never pay a broker's commission. There are 1,057 no-loads among the 6,090 mutual funds in Morningstar's database. There's always a no-load that's as good as or better than one with commissions. You can build your entire portfolio with no-loads.

Step 8: Keep it simple.
You need far fewer funds than you probably think. Studies suggest that 12 funds are enough for maximum risk protection. But when it comes to actual portfolio building, it varies. Some investment advisers recommend as few as six. Try keeping it to 10 or fewer.

Step 9: Stop playing with your portfolio.
Rebalancing a well-diversified portfolio more than once a year is a waste of your time and money. Behavioral finance professors Terry Odean and Brad Barber researched 66,400 investor accounts over a seven-year period and concluded that "the more you trade the less you earn." The returns of the passive investors were about fifty percent higher than the active traders, due to taxes and excessive transaction costs.

Step 10: Ignore the news.
Don't invest by what you read or see in the news. Buying or selling on breaking news is a loser's game. Markets are super-efficient; they react instantaneously to news, *before* you can boot up your computer or dial your broker.

Step 11: Don't believe people who "beat" the market.

Just as an alcoholic shouldn't hang around the local saloon, a recovering bull-market addict shouldn't swap too many stories with investors who brag that they are way, way up when the market is way, way down. At best, they are deluding themselves; at worst they are lying. Either way, don't let yourself go off the wagon and make more sucker investments.

Step 12: There's life beyond the market.

Remember, even in a bear market, someone's buying. You may be powerless over the market, but with steady savings, dollar-cost averaging, index funds and annual rebalancing, you will have plenty of power over your own portfolio and your life. The theme of the original 12-step program is "the joy of living." Same here.

About the Author
PAUL B. FARRELL, J.D., Ph.D.

Paul B. Farrell is a personal finance and investment columnist for DowJones-MarketWatch.com. He has published over 1,200 columns and frequently discusses the psychology, ethics and spirituality of money as well as practical everyday solutions. He is the author of eight books, including *The Millionaire Code: 16 Paths to Wealth Building, The Lazy Person's Guide to Investing, Mutual Funds on the Net, Expert Investing on the Net, The Millionaire Meditation,* and *The Winning Portfolio.*

Earlier Dr. Farrell was an investment banker with Morgan Stanley. He has been an executive vice president of the Financial News Network, where he was executive in charge of producing nearly a thousand hours of live cable television news; executive vice president of Mercury Entertainment Corporation, a publicly-held film production company; associate editor of the Los Angeles Herald Examiner; and executive director of the Crisis Management Group, counseling executives, entrepreneurs, politicians, healthcare professionals, athletes, rock stars, celebrities and royalty.

Dr. Farrell has four academic degrees: Juris Doctor, Masters in Regional Planning, Bachelors of Architecture, and a Doctorate in Psychology. He served in Korea with the United States Marine Corps, as a staff sergeant and aviation radar-computer technician. Today Dr. Farrell lives on the Central Coast of California with his wife, Dorothy, a psychotherapist.